Jess W. Curry, Jr., is a manager of management services for Arthur Young & Company and has fifteen years' experience in data processing. He holds a masters degree in computer science and is the co-author of *The ABCs of Microcomputers* (Prentice-Hall).

David M. Bonner is a senior management consultant with Arthur Young & Company. He holds a masters degree in accounting, is a certified public accountant, and has extensive experience in data processing.

HOW TO FIND AND BUY GOOD SOFTWARE

A Guide for Business and Professional People

Jess W. Curry
David M. Bonner

A SPECTRUM BOOK

PRENTICE-HALL, Inc., Englewood Cliffs, New Jersey 07632

Library of Congres Cataloging in Publication Data

Curry, Jess W.
  How to find and buy good software.

  "A Spectrum Book."
  Includes index.
  1. Computer programs—Purchasing.   I. Bonner,
David M.   II. Title.
QA76.6.C88 1983   001.64′25′0687   83-3014
ISBN 0-13-406660-X
ISBN 0-13-406652-9 (pbk.)

© 1983 by Prentice-Hall, Inc., Englewood Cliffs, New Jersey 07632.
All rights reserved. No part of this book may be reproduced in any form
or by any means without permission in writing from the publisher.
A Spectrum Book. Printed in the United States of America.

10 9 8 7 6 5

ISBN 0-13-406660-X

ISBN 0-13-406652-9 {PBK.}

Editorial/production supervision: Marlys Lehmann
Cover design © by Jeannette Jacobs
Manufacturing buyer: Cathie Lenard

This book is available at a special discount when ordered in
bulk quantities. Contact Prentice-Hall, Inc., General
Publishing Division, Special Sales, Englewood Cliffs, N.J. 07632

Prentice-Hall International, Inc., *London*
Prentice-Hall of Australia Pty. Limited, *Sydney*
Prentice-Hall Canada Inc., *Toronto*
Prentice-Hall of India Private Limited, *New Delhi*
Prentice-Hall of Japan, Inc., *Tokyo*
Prentice-Hall Southeast Asia Pte. Ltd., *Singapore*
Whitehall Books Limited, *Wellington, New Zealand*
Editora Prentice-Hall do Brasil Ltda., *Rio de Janeiro*

To Nancy and Susan

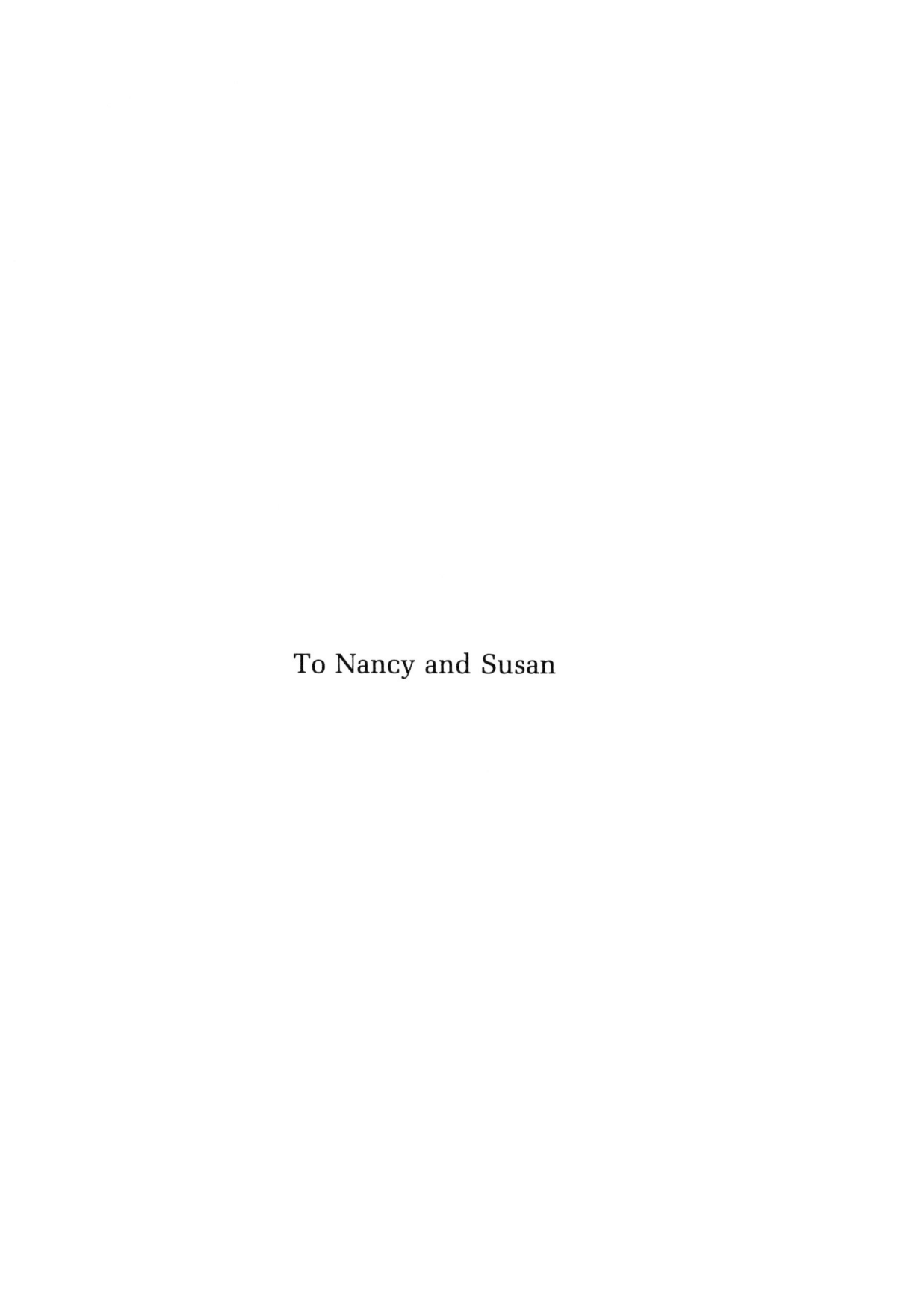

CONTENTS

Preface • ix

1
LESSONS FROM THE PAST • 1

2
THE EIGHT-STEP PROCESS: AN OVERVIEW • 11

3
IDENTIFYING YOUR NEEDS • 25

4
SURVEYING THE MARKET • 35

5
HARDWARE: A PRIMER • 43

6
UNDERSTANDING YOUR REQUIREMENTS • 55

7
LOOKING FOR VENDORS • 67

8
DOCUMENTATION: WHAT TO LOOK FOR • 75

9
HOW TO WRITE A VENDOR LETTER • 91

10
EVALUATING VENDOR RESPONSES • 99

11
THE DEMONSTRATIONS: WHAT TO LOOK FOR • 111

12
MAKING THE FINAL DECISION • 121

13
RECOGNIZING HIDDEN COSTS • 131

14
BOOKING YOUR INVESTMENT • 139

Glossary • 147

Index • 159

PREFACE

The advent of the microcomputer has opened new avenues for the small-business community. The proliferation of data processing in the small-business and hobbyist fields has not only increased hardware (equipment) sales and software (program) development, but has also served to increase the number of people learning to use a computer. Children are operating microcomputers in their schools, businesspeople are carrying computers in their cars, and homes are being inundated by personal computers for all kinds of uses. As the world becomes more familiar with the microcomputer, the mystique of computer jargon and acronyms is disappearing. Regardless of your background or education, the microcomputer has paved the way for a new revolution in information gathering and processing. This is a revolution that can greatly improve your business management and control.

The purpose of *How to Find and Buy Good Software* is to present in layman's terms a step-by-step procedure for purchasing a computer that meets your needs. Commonly used terms are defined in the glossary at the end of the book. These terms are italicized in the text. This book is the first in a series on managing small computer systems, each release of which is dedicated to providing the public with a guide to purchasing, installing, controlling, and managing a small-business computer. Although the examples and case studies are oriented toward the small-business community, *How to Find and Buy Good Software* will provide useful information to anyone who is faced with the computer-system purchase decision. Some of the other books in the series are: *The Microcomputer Implementation Cookbook*, and, tentatively titled, *Managing a Small Business Computer*, and *How to Evaluate Financial Systems*.

By following the advice contained in each volume, you will avoid many of the pitfalls that have befallen computer purchasers who have preceded you. This book presents an eight-step methodology which every purchaser should follow. The actual time dedicated to each step, however, should be in proportion to the total expected cost. Whether you are considering purchasing a small computer or you are just interested in learning more about their capabilities and limitations, *How to Find and Buy Good Software* is written for you.

ACKNOWLEDGMENT

We wish to express our appreciation to Diane O'Rourke for the artwork contained in this book.

LESSONS FROM THE PAST

It has taken the computer industry thirty-five years and at least four technological evolutions to reach the small-business community. In the 1950s and 1960s only the federal government and large corporations could afford a computer. In the mid to late 1970s the personal computer penetrated the homes of hundreds of thousands of people and educated the computer novice and hobbyist. The computer is no longer the mystic "box" understood only by the elite trained to speak in acronyms and computer jargon.

Under the pressures of increasing costs, growing competition, and, of course, continuing governmental regulations, the small-business community is changing. To keep a competitive edge, a business executive needs current, accurate, and meaningful information about his business and his competitors. For the first time powerful, cost-effective microcomputers are being built specifically for the small to very small business. More important, software programs are now available for even the smallest computer. These new developments can provide options to businesses without involving large investments. Computerization is sweeping the small-business community!

LESSONS TO LEARN

This does not mean that you can simply run down to your local computer store, pick up a nice-looking computer, and take it home as if it were a new car. This is in fact perhaps one of the biggest mistakes made today by small-business owners who want to automate. One businessman recalls a story of near nightmare proportions. Less than two years ago he visited a local computer store, and to his surprise, ended up buying a popular home computer with two small *floppy disk drives* and a *dot matrix printer*. The equipment cost $6,500. His objectives were clear. He wanted to operate the special programs the computer store had developed for small oil and gas producers. The man owned one large land lease with almost twenty wells already drilled. Easy enough, he thought. After all, the programs already work. Unfortunately he did not consider the other eighty wells he planned to drill on the same property. At forty wells he had to upgrade his equipment to six floppy disk drives, a commercial grade printer, and twice the memory capacity of his initial computer. These upgrades cost him an additional $7,000. At seventy wells a *hard disk* was required at a cost of $3,000. It was not until after his upgrade that he discovered that the purchased programs would not work with the hard disks. The new disk was easily installed and worked well with the computer. However, the oil and gas package did not work at all with hard disks. After $16,000 worth of contract programming the businessman gave up. The computer simply was not large enough to process his volume.

It cost this business executive $32,500 to window shop prior to planning. For an investment of $20,000 he could have had much more power, greater hardware growth capability, and far·fewer headaches.

This is a modern-day lesson—one that must be learned in light of the recent technological advances that make equipment available at such low prices. The $6,000 computer this man purchased may well solve the problems of many small businesses, but it did not solve his. Impulse buying and poor planning can be costly. This could not have happened in the 1950s, when computer costs were measured in millions of dollars. But there are many lessons, equally important, to be learned from the past. Indeed many mistakes being made today in buying the small computers are the same errors made ten, twenty, or even thirty years ago with the very large systems.

History tends to repeat itself. Before a business executive buys a computer system it is important that he or she have at least a general understanding of the trends of the computer industry over the past thirty years. Lessons can be learned from the past.

TRENDS OF THE 1950s

In the 1950s only the federal government and the largest of large corporations could afford the new and extremely expensive computers. In those days the cost of hardware equipment far outreached the cost of personnel. Data processing (D.P.) departments became people oriented as D. P. departments were established to provide programming for the large computer. In the early 1950s computer equipment was built primarily with vacuum tubes. These are referred to as the first generation of computers. The equipment was huge often requiring an entire floor of an office building. At Tinker Air Base in Oklahoma the first computers installed required hangar-size buildings.

In the beginning computers could perform only one process at a time. One senior analyst during the 1950s tells how he and other programmers would get access to the computer.

"In those days computer time meant the entire system was turned over (dedicated) to one programmer. The programmer would hand carry his punched cards into the computer room, where he would load them into the card reader, turn on the computer, and wait. There was no such thing as abort. When the computer found a program error it simply stopped. That's when we would pull out our latest development, the memory dump program. Of course everyone carried a punch card version of the program in his shirt pocket just in case. When the computer halted, the programmer had ten minutes to run his dump before the next programmer/analyst was called. Then it was back to the office to wade through stacks of computer paper filled with memory dumps."

Unlike today's high-level computer languages, systems in the 1950s were developed using machine-oriented computer languages. Large teams were required to develop even the simplest system and errors were often missed until long after the system was in use.

By the end of the 1950s the transistor became the main building block of the computer. These new systems were smaller and even cheaper, and were referred to as the second generation of computer hardware. Large manufacturing firms, banks, and insurance companies could now afford a computer and the data processing revolution moved into the mainstream of big business. The small businessman who could not afford the costly equipment or large development staff remained unaffected.

Managing a system during this period was not easy. Purchasing equipment was not a problem since there were only a handful of options. The difficulty arose in hiring, training, and managing large numbers of inexperienced people. Data processing was a new trade and tech schools and colleges offered little help. With so few machines sprinkled around the country, only a handful of experienced programmers and managers were available. Everyone had to be trained. As a result, major overruns were experienced on virtually every development project. Regardless of the project size, systems were rarely developed on time and within budget.

Two important trends developed during the the 1950s. These were:

- Data processing personnel developed a reputation for large project overruns, in both time and costs.
- The concept of buying hardware first then developing the software programs became the classic approach to computer automation.

In the beginning there were no *canned* or *packaged programs* from which a company could choose. The only option was to buy a computer, hire a mass of programmers, and begin developing the necessary systems. It would take at least two decades for the data processing industry to overcome its initial poor reputation in the area of overruns and almost thirty years before *software* would take precedence over *hardware* in the procurement process.

TRENDS OF THE 1960s

In the early 1960s the cost of equipment remained high, leading toward the trend to use a computer service bureau. There were hundreds of thousands of companies that could not afford a computer. As a result computer service bureaus sprang up all over the nation, offering the business community an opportunity to participate in the sharing of costs.

As this trend became more and more popular, the concept of sharing software developed and service bureaus began offering specific applications common to businesses. Programs for general ledger, accounts receivable, payroll, and so on were developed based on the concept of *shared processing*. These applications were trans*action driven* and cost effective compared to the price of a computer. Software became the selling point for deciding which service company to use. This trend played an important role in changing the direction of the data processing industry in the 1970s and 1980s, and for the first time some small businesses could cost justify automation through a service bureau.

In the late 1960s computer manufacturers began producing smaller computers, which eventually came to be called minicomputers. The concept of "bundling" became popular as manufacturers offered predeveloped software with the purchase of equipment. This made it difficult for new manufacturers to enter the market, since the cost of developing software continued to increase while hardware prices, and thus the cost of entering the hardware market, continued to fall.

During the 1960s operating systems and computer languages came into their own. Programmers were able to stop worrying about such tasks as how to transfer information from the computer to a disk drive, or how much data can be put on a disk. The operating system took over these tasks and allowed the programmer to concentrate on the end user. High-level, English-type computer languages made it possible for programmers to be more effective and efficient, and the number of people required to develop a system gradually declined. With large staffs being trained during the 1950s and reduced development time resulting from improved programming aids, data processing departments began searching for new projects. User awareness in the 1960s was on an upswing and the two groups began working together to identify new business applications for the computer. Unfortunately data processing's track record for providing timely, on-time project successes continued to be poor. D.P. management continued to underestimate project costs and development time, and often a user would not recognize the system once it was completed.

Industry trends changed in the following ways:

- The advent of the minicomputer reduced costs and more companies developed their own data processing departments.
- Service bureaus thrived by offering shared costs.
- The trend of buying hardware before the software continued, although software became a hardware selling point.
- Data processing departments continued the trend of running over cost and time budgets.
- Users began to play a more important role in all aspects of the data processing field.

Although D.P. problems continued to plague the business community, the industry showed signs of maturity. Better trained personnel were available, users started playing key roles, and hardware costs were dropping. The industry was growing and maturing rapidly.

TRENDS OF THE 1970s

The decade of the 1970s saw a computer revolution. The development of the microprocessor revamped the minicomputer market, and dozens of minicomputer manufacturers and OEMs (original equipment manufacturers) came into their own. Almost every large to medium, and many small businesses purchased computer systems. Successful systems development methodologies emerged from the 1960s, which improved the process by which systems were designed, developed, and installed. As a result, data processing successes became abundant.

By the end of the decade the microcomputer made home and personal computers a popular item, and retail computer stores began the process of educating the general public. Hardware costs declined radically, even on many of the large "maxicomputers." The automation of the general accounting functions became commonplace, and new users emerged who addressed more difficult business problems, such as optimizing human resources, improving management-decision tools, and direct user input through online applications.

Increasing personnel costs were offset by improved techniques and aids such as high-level languages like Pascal and BASIC. The concept of breaking tasks, projects, and assignments into manageable units became widespread and led to many successful projects. For the first time the trend of finding and buying software before purchasing hardware became a dominant theme. Only one major market remained largely unexplored: the small-business community.

TRENDS OF THE 1980s

From the beginning the direction of the 1980s was set: automate all small businesses. Almost immediately the price gap between the minicomputer, generally priced at $50,000 plus, and the personal computer, priced at $7,000 or less, disappeared. More important, programs were developed specifically for the small business. These systems provide menu-driven and user-friendly applications, which means that the operator's input options are displayed on a screen. Errors are caught immediately and the user can correct problems and data before the information enters the system.

The trends of the 1980s are taking form. To stay abreast of the competition small businesses will have to automate. Sound, cost-effective, and powerful computers are available. Business executives will select the software they need, then buy the computer necessary to operate the software. The market is being flooded with software packages and business computers. Hundreds of software products and computer models will spring up, and many, if not most, will disappear.

The computer systems of the 1980s will offer the business community new and exciting potential for improved operations, efficiency, and profits. Unfortunately it also offers new and potentially dangerous pitfalls that can devastate a small company's ability to compete in today's market. For the business executive of the 1980s, the key to success could well lie in his ability to purchase, install, and manage a useful and meaningful small-business computer. This does not require a technical computer expert as it did in the 1950s and '60s. What it does require is some technical knowledge on how to manage the important aspects of a computer system.

Lessons from the Past • **9**

This book will carry you through each phase, beginning with deciding what to automate (the needs analysis, discussed in Chapter 3) and ending with manual procedures and controls, which will keep your system operating effectively and under proper controls. We believe that with a little guidance and some good business sense you can install a computer system that will give you the competitive edge required to thrive in the 1980s.

GLOSSARY

Canned Package Self-contained programs that perform a specific function, such as payroll, accounts receivable, or accounts payable.

Dot Matrix Printer A printer that uses small dots to form characters. Generally less expensive and less durable than a standard printer.

Floppy Disk A thin, mylar, record-shaped disk housed in a protective cardboard jacket and used to store information and programs. Floppy disks have much less storage capacity than hard disks.

Hard Disk A standard, nonflexible and often self-contained disk, which can store from three million up to one billion characters of information.

Hardware The equipment and electrical components of a computer.

Memory Dump The procedure that allows a programmer to see portions of a program or data that are internal to the computer. Memory dumps are used by programmers to resolve programming errors.

OEM Abbreviation for original equipment manufacturer. OEMs are companies that buy and manufacture computer components and combine them into a marketable computer product.

Shared Processing Sharing the resources of a computer among two or more businesses.

Software The instructions that tell a computer what to do and how to do it.

Transaction Driven Computer software that is designed to create transactions that are later grouped or batched together to be processed by the next program.

THE EIGHT-STEP PROCESS: AN OVERVIEW

While there have been numerous articles written on how to buy software for a small-business computer, few have presented a systematic approach. Buying software for a large computer facility is considerably different from buying software for a mini- or microprocessor-based computer system. In a large facility the buyers are usually experienced computer technicians who understand all the jargon and buzzwords that have permeated the industry. In purchasing small systems the buyer is usually a businessperson or hobbyist who has little or no computer experience and whose expertise is in the various aspects of the business that the computer is expected to support. This can be a big advantage if the businessperson is willing to commit some preparation time to the first effort to buy software.

Other limitations in buying software for a small facility are the time and cost constraints. A larger facility may have a large budget and several months to properly define, search out, and acquire a computer package. The small-business owner needs to expedite the process without losing the quality necessary to insure that a meaningful and useful package is purchased. This can be done if the businessperson utilizes his or her knowledge of the business and takes a well-organized, systematic approach to purchasing software.

This book presents an eight-step approach to finding and buying good software. Some of the steps shown in Figure 2.1 are similar to those required by large facilities. However even these steps must be performed with a different perspective and with different constraints. The small-business owner, for example, simply does not have the time to perform an in-depth analysis of the business functions that will be automated. This is an important and necessary step in purchasing any computer software package.

In the small-business environment the owner, manager, or accountant who will be purchasing the software is generally well aware of the business functions to be automated. In the small-systems environment the objective becomes simply to document the business functions performed. This allows a vendor who is not familiar with the particulars of the business to understand the requirements of the system. No in-depth analysis is required, particularly if the buyer is already familiar with the business. If the person responsible for buying the software is not familiar with the business

FIGURE 2-1. The Eight-Step Process: An Overview

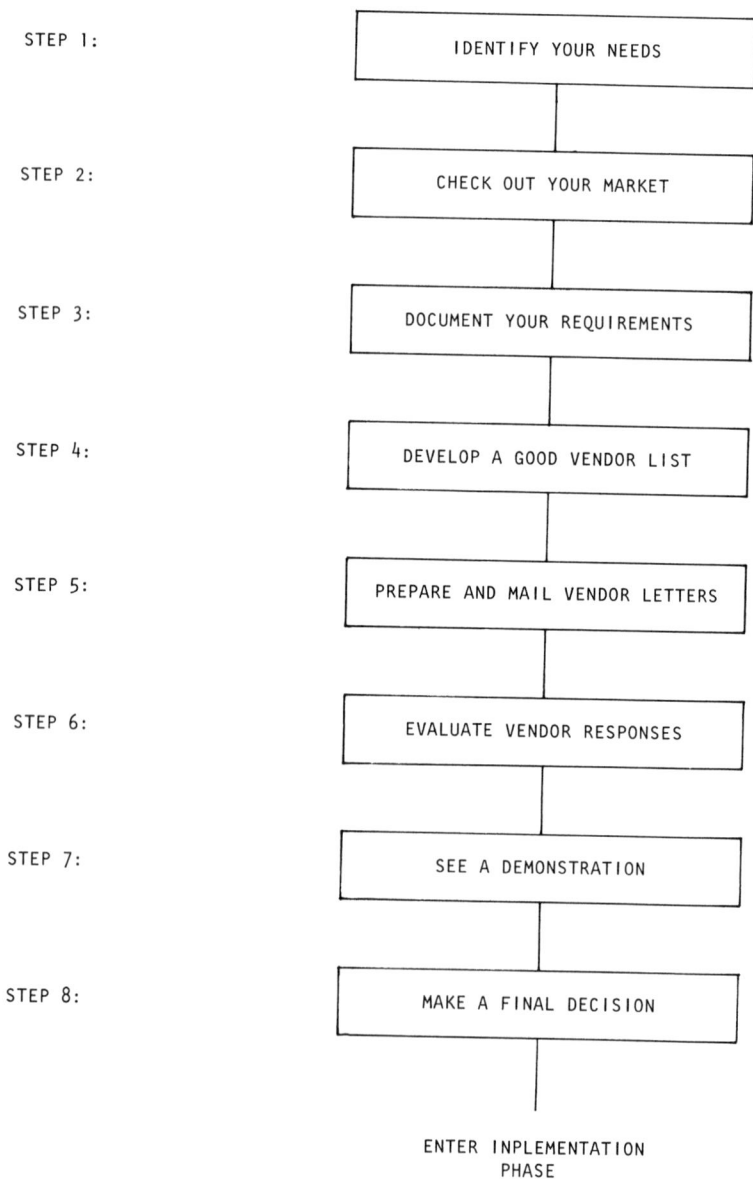

processes then it is best that someone else, who is involved with the process, be placed in charge of automating those particular functions. The production manager is not the person who should be buying a general ledger system. He may, however, be just the person to acquire a payroll package if the business function is oriented around the production process. This is an important ingredient that should be considered before the procurement process begins.

While some of the steps in the small-systems procurement procedures, such as preparing a requirements document and vendor letters, are modified versions of a large-systems approach, most are not. Where some steps could be modified to take advantage of the small-business owner's knowledge of the business, several new steps are required to familiarize the businessperson with the small-systems community. One of the objectives of the procurement procedure outlined below is to get the businessperson into a retail computer store at least three times. If this is the first time he or she has evaluated computer software, then three visits may consume more time than would be required in subsequent evaluations. This is true for each of the eight steps. Although each step is discussed in detail in the chapters that follow, the reader should keep in mind that the actual time allocated to each step will vary depending upon the system, the buyer's knowledge of the business functions to be automated, and, of course, his or her understanding of small-business computers. The remainder of this chapter is dedicated to giving a short overview of the entire small-systems procurement process. Detailed explanations, sample forms, and examples with case studies are given in each chapter. In general, however, the objective of this eight-step approach is to:

1. Understand what your requirements are
2. Become familiar with the small-systems marketplace
3. See demonstrations before you buy
4. Learn what type of questions are important to ask
5. Become comfortable in the small systems environment

There is one shortcut you should avoid. Once you are familiar with the small-systems market and have a good understanding of what can be expected from both the available hardware and software, do not start eliminating steps from the procurement process. Even though it may eventually take less time to perform a step, the step itself should be completed. It is important, for example, that you formalize your requirements even if writing them down only takes an hour. If you bypass this step you will encounter problems later in the process. Eventually, after you have gained experience with the methods involved, it may take as little as ten to fifteen hours spread over only a few days to find and buy a good *software package*. That is, once you know most of the vendors in your area and you are well aware of your requirements, it should take considerably less time to find and buy good software. Still, each of the eight steps should be performed. A small business can ill afford a $10,000 to $25,000 mistake that was caused by overconfidence.

STEP 1. IDENTIFY YOUR NEEDS

If this is your first effort to buy computer software, then identifying your needs is a particularly important step. The objective is to review your company's operation and identify which business functions potentially warrant automation. If in the past you have already automated one or more business functions and are aware of which functions you plan to automate next, then this step should be used to reevaluate the manual functions and identify which system best justifies the next automation project.

Once the business functions have been chosen, the next task is to study the functions separately and in detail, and to develop a list of processes that the purchased software should accomplish for you. Do not restrict your list; this list should represent your "nice-to-have" wish list. Later evaluation will restrict the list to those items that represent obtainable requirements.

STEP 2. CHECK OUT THE MARKETPLACE

Armed with your "nice-to-have" wish list the next step is to check out the marketplace by visiting several retail computer stores. This is not the time for a detailed evaluation of the vendors' software or for serious decision making. Instead, it represents an opportunity to ask questions about small-business computers and available software. It is a chance to meet several vendors in your area, to ask questions about the small-computer business in general, and to get a feel for what is available in the particular business area you have chosen to automate. For example, if you choose to automate your accounts receivable function, then use this trip to find out what is available for accounts receivable systems. What functions and processes are the systems performing and how do these functions fit into your "nice-to-have" wish list?

The main objective in this step is to become familiar with the general terms and expressions the vendors use, establish some level of expectation as to how well a small-system package would fit your business, and to become familiar with the types of software packages that are available. Generally at this stage it is considered better to visit several stores rather than spend a lot of time in only one retail outlet. General knowledge is the goal here, not specifics.

The final task in this step is to modify your wish list according to your improved knowledge of the small-systems marketplace. Your expectations, and thus your perception of your needs, should now be realistic as to what is available in small-business software.

STEP 3. DOCUMENT YOUR REQUIREMENTS

Once you have identified your needs and have visited several computer stores you should have a good feel for what your needs are and how well a software package can address those needs. The next step is to write down what the system must be able to do in order to meet your system requirements. For example, if you are searching for a payroll system, does the software need to have multistate deduction capabilities? How many people must the system be able to keep track of? Will departmental reports be required? The starting place for this document is your wish list. Eliminate the items you feel are no longer obtainable and provide further information for those that represent real requirements.

This is an important step that will play an invaluable role in your final decision. If you are weak in one or more areas of the business that require automation, seek help. Interview people in your company who know those areas and involve staff when necessary to get a clear picture of your actual requirements. The document you produce during this stage will be the key to your success in finding and buying a good software package. The document itself (referred to as the *requirements document*) does not need to be detailed. An outline with additional remarks for each item will do as long as it makes clear exactly what the requirements are. Whatever you do, make the requirements document a good and accurate description of your business's requirements. Otherwise you are in for a long and costly, and possibly misguided, procurement project.

STEP 4. DEVELOP A GOOD VENDOR LIST

The vendor list will also play an important role in finding and buying a good software package. Regardless of how well you have documented your requirements, if you do not have a good list of vendors to mail your requirements to, then you may never receive a responsive proposal from a reliable and supportive vendor. There are several good sources for vendor candidates. Computer magazines, especially those oriented to small computers, and business magazines in your field of business are excellent sources. Check the articles and the advertisements and begin a list of potential vendors.

Visits to the area computer stores are also a valuable approach to finding good vendors. If there are several stores in your area, then perhaps there are a few you didn't visit when you were surveying the marketplace (Step 2). If you have already visited all the stores around your town, then a second trip to a few shops is in order. On this trip, concentrate only on the software packages that meet your requirements. See a demonstration and try to narrow your expectations to the specific items in your requirements document. In the end you may need to improve your document, dropping requirements that vendors think are unrealistic and adding others they recommend. You may also get comments from the vendors that suggest new functions that the available applications can provide.

When this round of visits is over, you should be aware of what is being done in the particular business areas you plan to automate. By requesting a demonstration, you should have a good idea for how the systems will operate in your particular business environment.

STEP 5. PREPARE AND MAIL VENDOR LETTERS

At this point you may feel that you've already found exactly what you need. Stopping here is an option, but it is not recommended. As good as the system is, better systems may be available. The objective of this step is to find out if better systems are available.

Preparing a *vendor letter* amounts to preparing a cover letter for your requirements document, which was developed in Step 3. The letter should outline who you are, what you are doing, what cost limits you have, and under what deadlines you are working. Refer to the attached requirements document and be sure to give a specific date by which vendors should respond.

It is important that the letter outline for the vendor precisely how you plan to rate and choose the best system. How you choose to evaluate the software packages is especially important. Chapter 7 covers this topic in detail. However, the basic concept is to identify the characteristics that are most important to your business.

Examples of important evaluation criteria are:

- meeting the requirements outlined in the requirements document
- high-quality documentation
- availability of maintenance
- total cost
- what conversion assistance is offered

The next step is to weigh these facts by assigning them points based on their importance to you. The points should total 100. To simplify the evaluation process, create an *evaluation form* with a column for each of the characteristics to be graded and the weighting factors you chose for each. (An example is given in Chapter 10.) This form, or at least an explanation of the criteria with appropriate weights, should be included in your vendor letter. The letter must give a clear understanding of what the vendor is expected to do, and should detail when, and how, he will be judged.

The next step is easy. Mail the vendor letter and requirements document to every vendor on your list. If the letter is well written and clear, then you should not be interrupted by salespeople. Good vendors are experienced in responding to requests for proposals (RFPs), which is what you have produced. If a vendor feels he or she has a good software package to offer, then he or she will respond. Be sure, however, to give the vendor two weeks or more to prepare his or her best response.

STEP 6. THE EVALUATION PROCESS

As the vendors' responses start to arrive, take the time to scan each proposal closely. Don't evaluate it immediately. Simply check to see if there are any areas in the proposal for which the vendor has requested further information. If some clarification is needed, then call the vendor so he can respond quickly. If no action is required, set the proposal aside until the deadline you set in your letter for receiving proposals.

Give the vendors a day or so after the deadline before beginning the evaluation process. It is as much of an advantage to you to accept proposals arriving late as it is to the vendor whose response is delayed by the mail or who was a day late in mailing the response. When you start, first read each response. Make notes to yourself concerning your impression of the overall proposal. Don't worry quite yet about whether or not each system proposed fits your requirements. Be more concerned with the overall proposal and particularly how the various systems proposed fit together. When you finish, separate the proposal into the various systems being proposed. That is, make a separate stack for each system you have requested: general ledger systems, payroll systems, accounts payable, and so on.

The next step is to take one of the stacks and evaluate each proposed system by using your evaluation criteria and your requirements document. Make notes of particularly strong or weak areas and assign points (not to exceed that allowed in your criteria) for each evaluation factor. Sum the points for each system and rank the systems by the number of points earned. At this point use your own judgment to choose the best two or three proposed software packages for each system requested. You may choose packages from more than one vendor, but the common thread, at least, should be hardware. You may have to reject one of the best packages because the other systems have no acceptable proposal for that hardware. This is rare, however, since most vendors will propose a series of packages to fill all your needs and which can be executed on one or more brands of hardware.

Picking the finalists is a judgment call that only you can make. The objective is to pick two or three of the packages proposed for each system you require. Try to orient your choices around the hardware options. Pick the best candidates for each of two or three hardware options. You should consider the advantages offered by selecting a vendor with comparable packages. This is one reason that from this point on decisions should be based upon what hardware is compatible with the best overall software packages. Software is still the most important factor, but hardware should now be given heavy consideration.

Once you have made your decisions, let each vendor know whether he or she was chosen for the final evaluation.

STEP 7. GET A FULL DEMONSTRATION

It's now time to get serious about what you will buy. Call each vendor on your finalist list and arrange a demonstration for each system he or she has proposed. You should spend at least an hour on-site studying the system, watching it actually running, and executing it yourself. Put some new *master files* into the system (for example, customers) then enter several *transactions* against each master file. Get a good feel about the package by asking questions about weak areas you noted during your evaluation. Try to picture how the software would operate in your shop and ask pointed and serious questions. Don't let anything fly by.

Be sure to discuss and test any necessary automated *interfacing* between systems. If payroll, for example, is to automatically feed the general ledger, then have the vendor demonstrate the payroll system first, creating transactions that will be sent to the general ledger. If the vendor demonstrates the ledger system next, those payroll transactions should show up under the correct account. Doing this interfacing test is not always easy, but that's even better because you will get a good feel for the vendor's knowledge of the packages and his patience in seeing that it operates correctly. If he simply cannot get the interfacing right, then arrange to come back in a day or two. Automatic interfacing between systems could be very important to you. Don't let the vendor talk his way out of a key requirement, whether it be interfacing, maintenance, documentation, or whatever.

STEP 8. MAKING THE FINAL DECISION

After reviewing in detail the demonstrations for each of your final candidates, the decision should be relatively easy. Of the two or three candidates reviewed for each system, one will usually stand out. The difficulty at this stage comes from coordinating the decision around hardware. This is one reason why orienting your finalist list around hardware should help make the decision easier. The final decision is very judgmental. Which equipment offers the best software? Software must still be the dominating thrust, but hardware now begins to play a very important role. You need good, dependable, and reliable hardware that can supply the memory, speed, and storage capacities to meet your needs. Basic hardware considerations are given in Chapter 11.

BEFORE YOU BUY

Before you place your money on the table there are some financial considerations that you should consider. Can you claim an *investment tax credit*? How should you best finance the deal? What are some of the "hidden" costs? What are the important elements of the contracts? What will training cost? (There will always be some training costs, direct or indirect, perhaps both.) These and other topics are covered in the later chapters of this book. But first, of course, you must understand your company's needs, and Step 1 is the topic of the next chapter: "Identifying Your Needs."

GLOSSARY

Evaluation Form   The document used in the evaluation of prospective hardware and software suppliers.

Interfacing   When one software package prepares information in a format that can be used by another package without having to reenter the data through the keyboard.

Investment Tax Credit   The income tax credit that is allowed on the purchase of equipment used for business purposes.

Master Files   The data that is maintained on a computer system to provide a point of posting. For instance, the customer file is the master file for a sales system.

Requirements Definition   Statement of the requirements a business has for the performance of a computer system. See *Requirements Document*.

Requirements Document   A written document that contains the requirements definition. See *Requirements Definition*.

Software Package   Set of programs that interact to perform a predefined function. See *Software*.

Transactions Records containing new information about the master file data that are used to update the master file data. For instance, sales transactions are posted to customer master files on a computerized sales system. See *Master Files*.

Vendor Letter The letter a prospective buyer sends to a computer-system sales organization. The letter contains the specifics of the desired software and hardware along with guidelines for responding.

IDENTIFYING YOUR NEEDS

3

Deciding what to automate can be difficult even for a person experienced in data processing. There are, however, some general rules which lead to a successful result. These rules will assist you in developing a document called a *needs analysis*. The needs analysis outlines points about your business that are important factors in the purchase decision. It is the starting point for the requirement evaluation process, which is covered in Chapter 6.

UNDERSTAND YOUR BUSINESS CYCLES

The steps in applying the needs analysis concept vary depending on the specifics of a particular business. However, some basic procedures may be discussed and can then be adapted as needed. For instance, in most businesses there is a *sales/cash receipts cycle* in which a sale occurs, the sale is recorded, a bill is sent to the customer, and later a check is received and is posted against the original entry in the accounts receivable ledger.

Let's examine the other cycles that are commonly automated in a small business. These are the *purchases/cash disbursements cycle*, the payroll cycle, the inventory cycle, and the general ledger cycle. The purchases/cash disbursements cycle involves ordering items for sale or consumption, receiving the goods along with an invoice, recording the invoice, and subsequent generation of a check for the invoice amount. The payroll cycle begins with recording hours worked; next, a check-writing process occurs, along with the appropriate tax reports, and then the year-end tax reports are generated. The inventory cycle is a netting of the inflows of inventory items from the purchases cycle and the outflows of items from the sales cycle. Finally, there is the general ledger posting of miscellaneous items of small volume along with the monthly process of closing out the results of the other financial cycles.

As noted above, these groupings of activities into cycles are used because they describe the five "core group" functions performed by the typical software packages available from vendors:

- Sales/Cash Receipts Cycle = Accounts Receivable Package
- Purchases/Cash Disbursements Cycle = Accounts Payable Package

- Payroll Cycle = Payroll Package
- Inventory Cycle = Inventory Package
- General Ledger Cycle = General Ledger Package

The only divergence from these standards may occur in the payables and receivables software where industry-specific packages may replace the *generic packages*. This is because some industries have specialized information needs that are not met by standard software. In either case the information required in the *needs analysis* is the same.

As an example of the concept of cycles, consider the ABC Hardware Co., which is a small organization of forty-two employees in three stores. Owned and managed by Bob Jones, ABC is in the business of selling hardware parts through retail outlets. They buy items from manufacturers with whom they have continuing credit relationships. One person in each store is designated as a receiving clerk and checks merchandise as it is received. The bookkeeping department files receiving documents from the three stores and invoices by the date due to receive any discounts for early payment. They also post payments made to the general ledger, breaking down expenses by store and department. Involved in this payment process are other amounts due for such things as insurance, rent, and utilities. This sequence of processes is the essence of ABC's purchases/cash disbursements cycle. Similarly, the other cycles mentioned above can be found at ABC Hardware Co.

Mr. Jones has decided that it is time to consider a small-business computer. He hopes to accomplish three things. First, the burden on bookkeeping is at a point where the bookkeeper and her clerk fall behind at the end of the month, while they are not as busy during the month. Mr. Jones has heard that by using a computer, the workload can be spread out. This is accomplished by entering data throughout the month as it is received and letting the computer do the closing, billing, and check-writing processes. Second, he hopes to install a retail inventory method with minimal impact on his company. Finally, he would like to be able to get financial reports during the month without having to wait until the end of the month. Let's see how Mr. Jones can apply the concept of a needs analysis at ABC Hardware Co.

PERFORMING THE NEEDS ANALYSIS

A needs analysis is a process of answering the *what, where, when,* and *how much* of your business. To accomplish the analysis, you must take time to consider the critical factors in your business. Many times small-business owners have difficulty pinpointing specific information needs. This is because small businesses can often be operated without regard for management information. However, when considering a small-business system, you must be specific about your requirements.

Examining the *what* of a small-business system helps you to gain an understanding of the software products that are required. The process here is to look at your current operations with an eye toward both obvious and hidden requirements. The obvious needs are such things as financial statements, an aged accounts receivable listing, or a year-end payroll report. The hidden needs are those requirements that may not be readily apparent but which are necessary because of your other needs. In ABC Hardware Co.'s case, a requirement of the general ledger financial statements is for reporting by department within the store. Because of this, the accounts payable and accounts receivable systems that provide information to general ledger must have the ability to post invoices and payments by store number and department number. Thus the *what* becomes a list of required reports and screens and the data to be maintained.

The question of *where* information is used in a business must be considered both for *hardware* and *software* purchases. For example, the need for bookkeeping's access to *management information* at ABC Hardware Co. is important because of the number of phone inquiries. This dictates that two terminals be available so that phone calls can be answered at the same time as invoices are being entered. A second example is that the information that feeds the system, such as sales volumes, may be generated by a cash register. If tight inventory control is desired, *point-of-sale equipment* may be required. Another example is found in a small bank where encoded checks are being processed. Here, special reader-sorter equipment must be acquired. Finally, the information may be generated by salespersons in an out-of-town office. Depending on how critical the data is, special equipment and terminals may be required in the field.

The question of how critical the data is leads to the question of *when* is data important to a business. For ABC, several examples of this information can be found in the reporting requirements:

- When is a trial balance report needed?
- When does ABC close the monthly general ledger?
- When does bookkeeping write the checks?
- When should a customer appear on a past-due report?

The answers to these questions will lead to software requirements concerning the timing of processes.

The *how much* of a business environment takes two forms. First, in order to determine some of the characteristics of a software package, it is important to have an idea of field sizes you will require. Here, ABC must determine how large the general ledger account numbers should be, how large account balances are, and how many decimal places are necessary for percentage discounts. Mr. Jones wants a system that blends well with ABC's manual processees. This advantage is defeated if bookkeeping must use account numbers on the manual books that are different from those on the computer.

The second *how much* question concerns account and transaction volumes. As noted earlier, small-business systems are limited by physical constraints. By understanding the volumes of information required, a vendor can better help ABC to select the speed and capacity of the machine and the mass storage devices needed. On both of these *how much* questions, future growth is important, since, as was noted in Chapter 1, a system will quickly lose its effectiveness if it cannot meet growth requirements.

In examining the financial cycles mentioned above, the four standard questions of *what, when, where,* and *how much* must be answered for each cycle. As we have seen, this information is necessary in order to determine hardware and software requirements. A sample of a needs analysis for the ABC Hardware Co. is shown in the case study that follows. The case study includes all five of the cycles we have discussed, along with some typical answers to the four standard questions. It also describes how Bob Jones documented one of the cycles.

As you will see from this example, Mr. Jones has picked four of the five cycles as candidates for automation. The next step that Bob must perform is to define precisely what requirements on hardware and software are implied by the needs analysis. This process is described in Chapter 6.

ABC HARDWARE CO.—
NEEDS ANALYSIS

Mr. Jones began his needs analysis by studying the sales/cash receipts cycle. He asked the bookkeeper and the store managers *what* reports they needed and *when*. The first four reports listed in Table 3.1 are for bookkeeping and the *Past-Due Customer List* is for the store managers to use in deciding whether to extend further credit.

TABLE 3.1. ABC Hardware Co.—Needs Analysis

SALES/CASH RECEIPTS

Sales—approximately 200 per mo. entered by bookkeeper

Customer account #—6 positions, including 2-digit store code

Deposits—prepared 2 times per week and average 23 checks per deposit

Deposit vouchers—posted to A/R accounts once a week

Customer inquiries handled by bookkeeping

Screen inquiry needed—Account balance

Current A/R has 379 customers

Customer growth averages 14% per yr.

Reports needed—Aged A/R (monthly)
                Detailed acct. activity (weekly)
                Account balance list (monthly)
                Customer statements (monthly)
                Past-due customer list (monthly)

DECISION—Requires automation

From the bookkeeper, Mr. Jones received estimates on *how much* volume is currently processed as sales per month, checks per deposit, and customer accounts maintained. He also determined *how much* growth has been experienced in customer credit accounts and the size of the customer account number needed for future expansion.

Mr. Jones asked the bookkeeper *when* deposits are prepared and *when* the customer accounts are posted. He also asked both the store managers and the bookkeeper two *where* questions. One was where customer account inquiries are currently handled and where they should be handled in the future. The other question was where they would prefer that sales be entered into the new system. In both instances, the store managers and the bookkeeper agreed that bookkeeping should continue to handle the two processes.

The results of the inquiries that Mr. Jones made for the sales/cash receipts cycle can be seen in Table 3.1. Based on the number of transactions processed and the growth expected, the time required, and the reports generated, Mr. Jones determined that this cycle was indeed a good *candidate for automation*. A similar set of steps was followed for the other four cycles, and the documents can be seen in Tables 3.2 through 3.5.

TABLE 3.2. ABC Hardware Co.—Needs Analysis
PURCHASES/CASH DISBURSEMENTS

Invoices—vouchered as received

Vendor list—includes 184 vendors (little growth)

Vendor #—4 positions

Invoices—posted to A/P records by bookkeeper once a week

Inquiries—A/P balance handled by bookkeeping

Reports needed—Checks (monthly)
      Proof listing (monthly)
      Detailed vendor balance listing (monthly)
      Vendor alphabetical listing (monthly)

Invoices—average 103 per month

DECISION—Requires automation

TABLE 3.3. ABC Hardware Co.—Needs Analysis
INVENTORY

Inventory dept. #—2 positions

Inventory store #—2 positions

Transactions flow from A/P and A/R systems

Inventory posted—monthly

Budget totals updated—semiannually

Inquiry needs—none

Number of depts.—16

Department growth—small

Reports needed—Retail inventory method
      Acct. balance totals (monthly)
      Budget to actual inventory levels (monthly)

DECISION—Requires automation

TABLE 3.4. ABC Hardware Co.—Needs Analysis
PAYROLL

Employees—42

Checks—made out by hand

Inquiry needs—none

TABLE **3.4.** ABC Hardware Co.—Needs Analysis (cont.)

Reports needed—Checks (biweekly)
                    Proof listing (biweekly)
                    Year-end tax reports (yearly)

Growth—approx. 3 employees per year

DECISION—Do not automate

REASONS—Small number of employees
              Small number of documents generated
            Little growth to increase time spent by bookkeeping

---

TABLE **3.5.** ABC Hardware Co.—Needs Analysis

GENERAL LEDGER

G/L Acct. #—6 digits including
              2-digit store # and
              2-digit dept. #

G/L posted—end of month

Subsidiary systems—automatically feed G/L

Inquiry needs—none

G/L accts.—63

Separate journal vouchers—entered by bookkeeping

Reports needed—Trial balance (on request)
                    Balance sheet (end of month)
                    Store/dept. bal. sheet (end of month)
                    Income stmt. (end of month)
                    Store/dept. income stmt. (end of month)

Financial stmts.—prior yr. to current yr. comparisons

DECISION—Requires automation

GLOSSARY

Candidate for Automation A manual business accounting function, such as payroll or inventory, which is selected as a possible choice for automation by a computer-based system.

Generic Package A set of programs to perform a generalized accounting function, such as accounts payable, which does not have any industry-specific features. In other words, it will work generally well for most businesses but may not meet all the needs of any one business.

Hardware   The equipment and electrical components of a computer.

Management Information   Data belonging to the whole spectrum of information used by businesspeople in the performance of the business-management function. Examples include financial ratios, sales figures, personnel utilization, and equipment downtime.

Needs Analysis   Document prepared as an initial step in the process of procuring a small-business computer system. The purpose of this document is to identify business-information requirements that may justify automation.

Past-Due Customer List   Report showing customers who are past due in paying off an account receivable. The report shows the amount categorized by how late the payment is and any partial payments received.

Point-of-Sale Equipment   Equipment used to receive sales information at the time it occurs (for instance, at the cash register). This is in contrast to waiting until the end of the day to enter sales information using accumulated sales slips or other documents.

Purchases/Cash Disbursements Cycle   The business cycle in which a purchase is made, a bill is received, an account payable is recorded, and finally the payable is reduced or eliminated when payment is remitted to the seller.

Retail Inventory Method   An accounting process for inventory valuation and sales cost calculation which works on an average cost basis. This method starts with a base ratio of sales price to cost and uses that to estimate the cost of goods sold given total sales at retail.

Sales/Cash Receipts Cycle   This term refers to the business cycle in which a sale is made, an account receivable is recorded, and (hopefully) cash is received to eliminate the receivable.

Software   The instructions that tell a computer what to do and how to do it.

SURVEYING THE MARKET

4

"I know what I want, but I just can't talk with those computer people." How often that comment is made! The speakers come from a variety of backgrounds but share a common frustration with the confusing language of the computer industry. All too often the result of this frustration is to give up on automation. It is unfortunate that the technical nature of computers makes some jargon necessary. Otherwise, the complications involved could not be adequately communicated. However, there is no reason why a small-business owner, who has mastered the complexities of the modern business world, cannot also overcome computer jargon.

This chapter will describe a three-step approach to mastering the mysterious language that people who work with computers use. The intent of this approach is to provide useful knowledge while keeping the reader from having to become a computer expert. The first step is to spend a few hours browsing through some small-business computer magazines. Next comes your homework—spending time reviewing a good book or two on the subject. This chapter will describe a method to make the work as painless as possible. Finally, the prospective small-business system purchaser must brave the elements and visit a computer store. Again, there are some things you can do to make the visit productive.

To effectively use this chapter, it will first be necessary for you to take inventory of your computer knowledge. This chapter and the next are structured to be a unit on the basics of small-business computers. The three-step process for gaining an understanding of computers and the jargon that surrounds them is outlined below. Chapter 5 provides some basic concepts of small computers and explains what areas you should not worry about if you don't understand them. If you already have some experience with small-business computers (hopefully from successful experiences), then you can safely skip to Step 3 and pay a visit to your computer store. Before you do, however, you should review the next chapter to make sure that you are familiar with all of the terms. If you are not comfortable in the presence of daisy wheels and K's, then do not try to skip ahead. A little time spent reading Chapter 5 and finding other articles on hardware can save you much grief later on in the process.

The first step in the three-step process for becoming familiar with computers is to learn what is available on the market. One approach is to begin by browsing through a few of the many small-business and personal-computer magazines that carry articles and ads on what is available. Such magazines can be found in most libraries and are often sold in bookstores. There are three points to watch for when you look through these magazines:

- What types of hardware are available on the market?
- What buzzwords are being used?
- What software might be useful given the needs you have previously identified?

Do not expect to become an expert after one reading of a microcomputer magazine. The point is not to become proficient, but rather to become familiar. To that end, read what you can, write down questions about what is confusing, and skip the technical articles, especially those concerning microelectronics and programming. Instead, read articles about hardware, software products, and "how tos" dealing with buying and using microcomputers.

The second step in becoming familiar with small-business systems is to gain a general understanding of the terms of the industry. To do this you will have to buy one or more ABC books on the subject. You should be selective at this point. For instance, avoid books on specific computer systems, those on how to do BASIC language programming, or ones with listings of specific computer programs. The books you are looking for go through the components of a microcomputer and detail the functions and features of each. The next chapter gives an overview on the subject of hardware. Read it first, then buy several small books on the topic. Again, do not worry if you do not understand every concept. There are many facts about microcomputers that are not necessary for you to understand to make a good small-business system purchase. Also, the terms will make more sense when you see your first microcomputer. Table 4.1 contains a list of terms you should understand before venturing into a computer store. When you are familiar with these terms, you will be ready to see a computer in action.

The first visit you make to your local computer store should be to gain a feel for how a microcomputer looks and performs. This initial visit has no real purpose other than to gain that familiarity. In fact, if you know someone with a small-business computer system, having them show it to you will serve a similar purpose. Try to remember some of the types of hardware that you have been reading about and look for them in the store. This initial visit may even be made to look for one of the ABC books mentioned in the previous step. In any case, just browse around and try to avoid the salespeople.

TABLE 4.1. Hardware Terms to Understand (Covered in Chapter 5)

1. CRT or Monitor
   - high and low resolution
   - graphics
   - 40 and 80 column
2. Keyboard
3. CPU
   - peripherals
   - K or Kilobytes
   - RAM
   - ROM
4. Printer
   - CPS
   - LPM
   - dot matrix
   - daisy wheel
   - letter quality
   - single sheet feed
5. Disk Drives
   - floppy disk
   - hard disk
   - Meg or Megabytes

After you have seen the store and feel comfortable with computers, contact a vendor and arrange a demonstration where you can see some software in action.

An initial demonstration is your first contact with a potential computer system. If possible, you should arrange for a demonstration of a type of software that you intend to consider. You should realize one thing about this demo. That is that you will be receiving the vendor's demonstration during this initial presentation. Whether the show is in a store or at some customer's office, the vendor will be planning to show the best parts of his software and will arrange the demo so that these stand out. Since this is to be expected, turn it to your advantage.

By allowing the vendor to give you "his" demonstration, you can avoid a major commitment at this stage in the selection process. After all, you have not even defined your requirements yet. The needs analysis and the question list you prepared while doing your reading provide a means of knowing what questions to ask. Do not get too involved in details at this stage, but make sure that you get all of your questions answered. Also, note your general impressions of the software being demonstrated:

- Was the system easy to use?
- Did the screen messages make sense?
- Are the reports meaningful and neatly laid out?

The information you gained from your needs analysis questions and from your general impressions of the software and hardware give you a sufficient level of understanding at this point.

If you like the software you see and feel that it may meet some of your needs, tell the vendor that you will send a request letter outlining the details of your requirements. Let him know your timetable so that he realizes you are a serious customer. Also, ask for a contact person for the letter. In many organizations the demonstrator cannot quote prices. The contact person will also be used for questions which will inevitably come up during the later stages of your evaluation.

Once you have seen a first software demonstration, it is time to begin your list of possible vendors. This vendor list should include all potential sources. In a later chapter you will perform a search for all possible vendors, so here you begin to list any potential sources of software you find during an initial demonstration. Don't worry about the size of the list at this juncture; you want a large list in the beginning. The more vendors on the list, the easier comparisons become. It is after the vendor letters have been sent out and the responses have been received that you will begin narrowing down the list. Even noncontenders provide a service by giving you a view of the areas in which the current market may not satisfy your needs.

For every vendor you put on your list, note your impressions. To do this the list must be kept current and added to after every demonstration. The comments should include both good and bad points about the software. Your notes on what you found in the market will help both as you prepare your requirements documents and later, when the vendor letters are drafted. One client was given a demonstration for some software that he was interested in, but unfortunately the software was priced and targeted for a much larger organization than the client's business. The client's comments on his evaluation sheet were "great software, meets many needs, priced much too high for us."

TABLE 4.2. Initial Vendor List

Vendor	Comments	Hardware Supported	Operating System
Computer Inc.	Saw General Ledger and Accts/Payable. Both were easy to use and look good.	Micro-Gamma	CP/M
The Computa Store	Only had General Ledger. Very hard to use and difficult to input data. They would like to propose. We need to send them a Vendor Letter.	Computa-1 & Computa-2	Computa-Soft

    Two columns to be included on your vendor list are "Hardware Supported" and "Operating System." The first of these questions concerns the hardware on which a vendor's software package will run. It is a common misconception that packages can run on any computer system. Unfortunately the physical characteristics of each small-business computer are unique enough that software must be tailored to an individual machine. Most software companies choose a popular computer line and design software for that system. Then if their software is successfully marketed they will consider investing the time necessary to make versions available that will run on other computer models. As you can see, this is an important fact to include on your vendor list.

    An *operating system* is simply a set of programs that handles the translation of program commands into physical commands. It is, if you will, the bridge between the programmer's logic and the computer's electronics. This is an important point to consider when evaluating software products. As you saw above, every computer has unique hardware characteristics. One way in which the problems inherent in this approach can be overcome is to have an operating system that is widely accepted by many hardware vendors and can thus provide a universal bridge to various computers. Then when you outgrow one computer system you need not necessarily throw away the software. The operating system closest to this ideal is one called *CP/M*. It is widely accepted, although not entirely *hardware independent*. CP/M-based software is available on a variety of computers.

An example of a vendor list that Mr. Jones started during his survey of the market is presented in Table 4.2. The list is not long, as Bob visited only three computer stores. It is a list that will be added to as he begins the vendor search process. Before spending any more time looking for vendors, Mr. Jones knew that he must complete the definition of his requirements. This is the next step in the process of finding and buying good software, and is the subject of Chapter 6.

GLOSSARY

CP/M A computer operating system that is widely used and accepted among microcomputer manufacturers. The advantage of a CP/M-based system is that there is a large variety of software available that executes under the CP/M operating system.

Hardware Independent A term used to refer to software that can be run on any machine without having to be modified. True hardware independence is very rare because of the lack of uniformity among hardware manufacturers.

Operating System The special set of programs and utilities that control the various parts of the hardware and make it operate as a unit. The user's application programs execute under the control of the operating system. For example, when a program prints a line, the function is performed by the operating system, which executes the actual printing at the request of the application program.

HARDWARE: A PRIMER

5

What are the important components of a small-business computer? How do computers work and what do you look for when you purchase one? These are questions asked by many businesspeople faced with the purchase of their first small-business computer. A local businessman in the construction trade decided that the best way to understand computers was to visit a computer store and learn about them firsthand. This would have been a good decision if he had done his homework first. To begin with, the businessman had not taken a look at what was available. His second mistake was that he was not familiar with the computer stores in his area, and as a result he ended up visiting a store that specialized in personal computers rather than small-business systems. As a result, when he arrived at the store he was at the mercy of a salesman, who sold him a personal computer that was too small for his business. The system had to be scrapped less than a year later.

How do you avoid having the same problems? In the previous chapter, "Surveying the Market," you read about a three-step process for becoming familiar with computers. The second step in this process was to understand the buzzwords that are associated with computers. Becoming aware of what is available on the market is something you would certainly do if you were buying a car for your business. Similarly, there is no substitute for being an informed shopper when looking for a small-business system. In this chapter you will be given an overview of the essential components of a small-business computer and will learn which facts are important to understand and which can safely be forgotten. A special glossary of hardware terms has been added at the end for quick reference.

To begin a discussion of the components of a small-business computer, it is necessary to first describe the computer as a whole. Figure 5.1 is a diagram of a typical small-business computer. It should be understood that for various reasons the computer you see at a store may not look exactly like the one in the diagram. However, the five major components of a computer can almost always be found:

- CRT (Cathode Ray Tube or "monitor")
- Keyboard
- CPU (Central Processing Unit)
- Printer
- Disk drives

FIGURE 5–1.

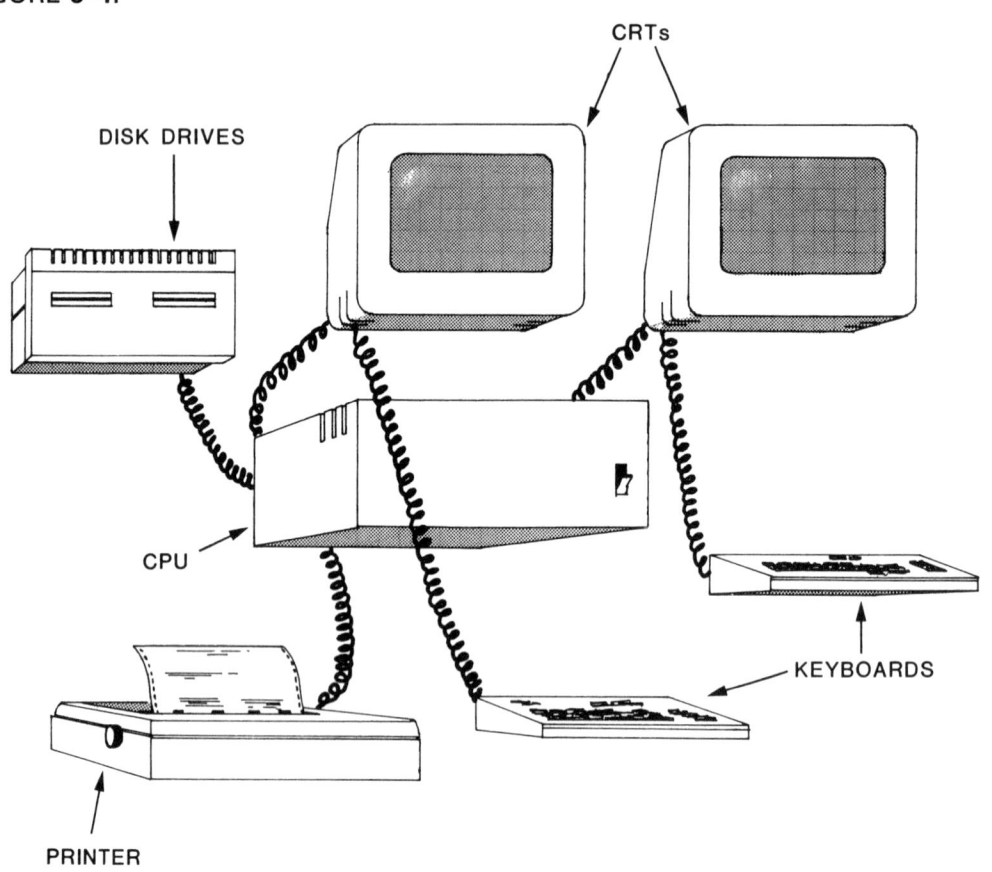

Hardware: A Primer • **47**

As you can see, there are a few things to learn just to understand the five basic buzzwords that describe a small-business computer. The following sections go into more detail about each area, but don't let that deter you from reading on.

THE CRT

The *CRT, monitor,* or *terminal* is the device that allows you to communicate with the computer. A CRT should be thought of as a specialized TV set, since it has no intelligence and displays exactly what it receives from the CPU. In fact to reduce cost, some personal computers use home TVs in place of the CRT. You want a monitor dedicated to your business, however, since using a TV in its place is unacceptable for most business environments.

There are just a few basic facts that you should understand about CRTs. First, there are several different types of monitors. There are multicolored monitors and monitors that display green letters on a black background (green is easy on the eyes). There are monitors that display 40 characters across the screen and those that display 80 characters. Finally, there are monitors that have the ability to show detailed figures and graphs because they have more "dots" on the screen. These monitors are said to have *high resolution*. A *low-resolution* monitor can still show graphs, but they are not as clear and detailed. Low-resolution monitors are fine, however, if you work mainly with words and numbers.

How do you choose a monitor? Mainly you apply common sense to your business environment. Unless you have a need to draw color diagrams on your monitor, for instance if you are an engineer, then you probably do not need a color or high-resolution CRT. The 80-column option may be necessary if you are a financial planner who works with large spread sheets. If you cannot think of a reason why you would need one of the specialized monitors, then save yourself some money and stick with a more common CRT. The primary point to consider when choosing a CRT is the vendor's experience with maintenance. You want to shop for a monitor that will not spend much time being serviced, just as you would a TV set.

KEYBOARD

The keyboard is the easiest item to understand, since it is like a typewriter keyboard. There are only a few options available on most

48 • *Hardware: A Primer*

keyboards. Try out the keyboard when the computer is demonstrated. Is it comfortable to the touch? Someone will be spending a lot of time using it. Avoid keyboards that have keys like calculators. Small keys are less comfortable to use and usually mean that you are looking at a lower-cost personal computer rather than a small-business computer. Some of the options available are lower-case letters and number-entry pads.

The lower-case option is often unnecessary. Most computers display screens in upper case. If you plan to use your computer for word processing—to create letters—then the word processing software should handle the upper- and lower-case letters without having a special keyboard. The number-entry pads are special keys on the keyboard that are arranged like those on an adding machine. These are useful if you plan to enter a large amount of numeric data, but they add to your cost and are certainly not essential.

CPU

The central processing unit is the "brain" of the computer. Here is contained all of the microelectronics necessary to make the computer work. In fact, all the devices that are attached to the central processing unit are referred to collectively as *peripherals* implying that they are outside the heart of the computer. There are many buzzwords that apply to the CPU, but you need to understand only a few when buying a small-business computer. The first concept to understand is that of a K. The K stands for *kilobyte*, which is approximately 1000 characters of storage. The significance of this concept is that the number of kilobytes or K's of storage that your computer contains determines how large and how complicated a program it can handle. In fact, any program you might buy will tell you the type of computer it can be processed on and the K requirements. As an example, small personal computers typically have 8, 16, or 32 K of storage available. In contrast, small-business computers may have 64, 128, or 256 K of memory (note that memory and storage are used interchangeably). As you might expect from these numbers, a small-business computer is capable of running larger and more complicated programs than is a personal computer. The fact that determines how much K you need for your small-business computer is the highest K requirement of all the software you expect to run on the computer.

Another concept that you should be familiar with but need not totally understand is that of *RAM* and *ROM*. RAM stands for random access memory and ROM is read only memory. Both are stated in terms of Ks. The RAM is used when application programs are run. For example, if you buy a general ledger program it will run in RAM storage. The ROM storage is used by the computer to store all the instructions it needs to make your system run. It is not available for other uses so you need not be concerned about how much ROM your computer has. Let the computer manufacturer worry about that. Unfortunately, many manufacturers decide to tell you the number of K for both types of storage in their brochures, so consider only the RAM number.

As a final point concerning central processing units, let's discuss some other facts you can safely ignore when the salesperson talks to you (although you might want to nod knowingly). The first is the type of microprocessor, which means the type of electronic hardware inside the CPU. Unless you are an electrical engineer there is no reason why you should be concerned. A second point frequently brought up is the number of ports. A *port* is a buzzword that denotes the CPU's access to all of the other peripheral devices we are discussing. You do not have to worry about this as long as you tell the salesperson the largest number of printers, disk drives, and terminals you will need to attach to your computer. Let him handle the rest.

PRINTER

A *printer* is a typewriter with some special electronics added to allow it to receive its keystrokes from the central processing unit. There are several points to understand about printers, but fortunately none of them is very complicated. The first point to consider is the speed of your printer. The central processing unit can run very quickly, usually much faster than the printer can print, so a printer normally runs near its maximum rated speed. Printer speeds are stated in terms of characters per second (CPS) or lines per minute (LPM). The speed that a printer needs to have to be adequate for your business depends on the type and amount of printing you intend to do. For instance, if you plan to do a high-volume label or invoice printing, then you need a fairly fast printer rated in lines per minute. On the other hand, if you plan only to print a small number of reports for your own use, then a slower printer rated in characters per second may be adequate.

There are two primary types of printers. One type, known as a *dot matrix printer*, makes characters by using a series of dots

FIGURE 5–2.

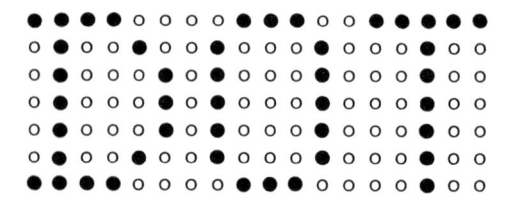

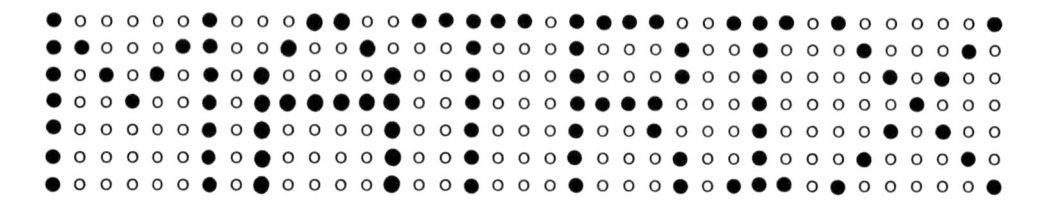

(see example in Figure 5.2). This is an easy process mechanically and therefore relatively fast dot matrix printers may be purchased for a reasonable price. Unfortunately, many people object to having to read the lettering created by a dot matrix printer. The second type of printer creates characters that look typewritten. The most common means of accomplishing this is through the use of a print *daisy wheel*, in which the letters are on spokes of a wheel, much like the petals on a daisy. Daisy wheel printers are slower than their dot matrix counterparts, and because of the number of mechanical parts involved, they also tend to be more expensive. A daisy wheel printer may also have *single-sheet* page feed to allow you to use typewriter paper rather than the standard *perforated computer paper*. The issue that normally is the deciding factor in whether to choose a dot matrix or a daisy wheel printer is whether you will be printing documents that require a typewritten appearance.

There are just a few more points of discussion concerning printers. First, be aware of the noise generated by any printer you see demonstrated. Daisy wheel printers tend to be noisier than dot matrix printers, but some manufacturers have done a better job of noise control than others. Also, stay away from printers that use special thermal paper. The documents created by a *thermal printer* feel uncomfortable to the touch, and besides, a computer with this type of printer is probably a personal rather than a small-business computer. Finally, some printers have *enhanced graphics* and multicolor capabilities. Just as with graphics monitors, the deciding factor should be whether or not you do much graphic or figure creation in your business. If you do not, then save yourself some money and stick to a basic character printer. You can still do graphics, although not quite as well.

DISK DRIVES

A *disk drive* is a device that allows you to use permanent storage disks. An analogy frequently used is that the drive is like a phonograph and the disk is like a record. Just as information is stored on the record and comes to life when the phonograph is turned on, so it is with disks and drives. When a computer is first turned on for the day, it has no application information stored within it. You must "play" some type of program disk and load the instructions to make it perform. Disks then contain program instructions, and in fact whenever you buy an application package such as a general ledger system, you will receive a disk with the program instructions contained on it. Another use for disks is storage of data. The general ledger system, after a period of some months, will have accumulated a large amount of posting history. Since the computer loses all knowledge when it is turned off, the logical place to store this history is on a disk.

Because they are required to store such large amounts of information, disks typically have much greater storage capacities than CPUs. The primary type of disk available in today's microcomputers is known as a *floppy disk*, because it is flexible. Floppy disks can be interchanged in a disk drive, so that when one disk is full, you can enter a new one. As you will remember, CPUs have storage rated in Ks, or approximately 1000 character storage units. Floppy disks for some computers have storage rated in Ks, but there are some larger floppy disks with ratings in the million-character storage rank known as Megs. If this is all very confusing, don't be alarmed. Your salesperson should be able to advise you concerning the amount of storage that you need. All you should know is that a Meg is a thousand times larger than a K, and that the larger the capacity of your disks, the less often you will have to stop and change disks.

Another point about disk drives concerns the equipment necessary to make a disk drive work. The buzzwords that are associated with disk drives include *peripheral interfaces* and *controllers*. It is not important that you understand the functions these devices perform, but you should know that they can add to the cost of your system. Depending on the way your computer is designed, it may require some combination of hardware and software to make the disk drive work, and these items may appear as separate items on the vendor's price list. Be sure that you ask the vendor for the total cost of hardware and software required to have a working disk drive unit.

Finally, there are some disk drives known as hard disks, which have the capacity to store information in the 10 to 50 Meg range. That is a lot of information! These disks are not interchangeable, but with the storage capacities involved, interchanging them should not be required. The hard disk is more expensive than a floppy disk drive, but may be necessary if you need to store large amounts of information and do not want to have to be constantly interchanging disks. Most hard disk units need a floppy disk drive, a *magnetic tape*, or cassette drive to provide backup in case the hard disk has a mechanical failure. You cannot afford to replace 50 million characters of information!

POSTSCRIPT

As a final note about hardware, be aware that although most manufacturers make all of the devices we have talked about, it is also possible to substitute hardware. There are many companies making specific devices, for instance terminals or disk drives, that are directly compatible with the major brands of hardware. Your vendor should be able to advise you as to what is available. The only concern you should have is that the substitutions you make have no effect on your warranty or the computer's reliability.

In the next chapter you will begin the process of documenting the specific software requirements of your business. That set of specifications will later become the determining factor in choosing hardware.

GLOSSARY

Controller A controller is a hardware device that is used to control the communications between the computer and one or more peripheral devices. Information sent to a peripheral is intercepted by the controller and translated and timed so that the peripheral can be operated more efficiently.

CPS An abbreviation for characters per second. CPS is a measurement of the speed at which a printer operates. For example, 30 CPS is considered slow. See *LPM*.

CPU An abbreviation for central processing unit. The CPU is the "brain" of the computer in that it is the hardware that performs the arithmetic and logical functions.

CRT Abbreviation for cathode ray tube, which is a peripheral device resembling a television and is used to display input and output information and data.

Daisy Wheel A circular printing device that is used on many printers to give the printer letter-quality capabilities. A daisy wheel printer is usually more durable and expensive than a dot matrix printer.

Disk Drive A peripheral device that spins a record-type disk and stores and retrieves information on the disk's platter. The platter can be hard or flexible. See *Hard Disk* and *Floppy Disk* in final glossary.

Dot Matrix Printer A printer that uses small dots to form characters. Generally less expensive and less durable than a daisy wheel printer.

Enhanced Graphics A printer or printing device that can print detailed graphs, often in color.

Floppy Disk A thin, mylar, record-shaped disk housed in a protective cardboard jacket and used to store information and programs. Floppy disks have far less storage capacity than hard disks.

High Resolution A characteristic of a terminal device (CRT or printer) that allows it to print enhanced graphics because it enables it to print more dots in each character's dot matrix than can a low-resolution dot matrix device. See *Dot Matrix Printer*.

K An abbreviation for kilobyte.

Keyboard That part of a peripheral device that is styled like a typewriter and is used to key information into the computer.

Kilobyte A unit of measure which equals 1024 bytes; is primarily used to describe internal or external storage capacities. See *Byte*.

Low Resolution A terminal device (CRT or printer) that cannot print as many dots in a character's dot matrix as a graphics or high-resolution dot matrix device. See *Dot Matrix Printer*.

LPM An abbreviation for lines per minute. LPM is a measurement for the speed at which a printer can operate. For example, 100 LPM is considered slow for a line printer.

Magnetic Tape Peripheral-storage device utilizing magnetic tape as the medium. This is usually found on small-business computers only as a way of backing up large hard-disk storage devices. See *Hard Disk and Peripheral*.

Meg A term for megabytes, or one million bytes of information capacity.

Perforated Paper Special printer paper that is perforated so that it can enter the computer as a continuous sheet and can be bursted into single sheets after printing. Perforations along the outside edges are often used to allow special pin-feed holes in the paper that the printer uses to feed the paper into the printer. With the perforations the pin-feed holes can be torn off.

Peripheral A device that is external to the main frame of the computer. Generally peripherals are used as input or output devices such as printers, CRTs, and disk drives.

Peripheral Interface See *Controller*.

Port An electrical outlet that the computer uses to pass information from the mainframe to the peripheral devices.

Printer A peripheral device that is used to make printed copies of information in the computer.

RAM An abbreviation for random access memory.

ROM An abbreviation for read only memory.

Single Sheet Feed A printer that can print on standard paper that is not perforated and is not continuous. See *Perforated Paper*.

Terminal A peripheral device that can serve as an input device (card reader) or an output device (printer) or both (CRT).

Thermal Printer. A printing device that uses a special heat-sensitive paper. Thermal printers are generally cheaper but the thermal paper required is more expensive than standard computer paper.

Magnetic Tape Peripheral storage device utilizing magnetic tape as the medium. This is usually found on small-business computers only as a way of backing up large hard-disk storage devices. See *Hard Disk and Peripheral*.

UNDERSTANDING YOUR REQUIREMENTS

6

As you saw in Chapter 3, the first step in automating a business is to determine what business functions could benefit from automation. To address this question a needs analysis is performed and a list of candidates for automation is developed. At this point the list of candidates represents the company's "wish list." Although you have taken a quick look at the market, there is no guarantee that software can be found that will fulfill the company's needs. In fact, the needs analysis has not identified exactly what it is that each application must do in order to meet the company's needs. The high-level, almost cursory nature of the analysis prohibits such detailed results. The purpose of the wish list is to limit the more detailed follow-up review to those business functions that are best suited for automation.

Recently a candy distributor spent a full day developing a list of automation candidates. The next day he rushed out to a retail computer store and presented his list to the store manager. Of course, the store had exactly what the distributor needed—a general ledger, inventory, and a payroll system. The distributor purchased the package. It wasn't until the candy distributor's accountant arrived that the distributor discovered his error. The payroll system did not have a multistate capability, the general ledger was single-entry rather than double-entry, and the inventory system used an average costing algorithm rather than actual costs. The distributor had purchased $4800 worth of useless software. Even though he had performed the needs analysis well and had correctly identified his system needs, the needs analysis did not insure that the software the candy distributor bought would satisfy the company's data processing needs.

The needs analysis is meant only to find candidates, not to define specific requirements. To purchase or even to develop a system based solely upon the results of a needs analysis can be a costly mistake. As the candy distributor discovered, what is needed is a definition of how each system or business function must operate in order for the software to meet the company's needs. This information is acquired through a second review called the *requirements definition*.

The requirements definition is not a complicated process, but it does require a thorough understanding of each business function being considered. Where the needs analysis for a small business may be performed in a few hours by the owner, controller, or accountant, the requirements definition usually requires the knowledge of several individuals and should, by nature, take longer to develop. Only one person, however, should be responsible for defining the software requirements. This individual should interview those employees who are most familiar with the current business processes. From these interviews the person responsible will develop a uniform set of minimum requirements, which will become the requirements documents for the software being considered.

Obviously the amount of time and effort required and thus the number of people assigned will depend upon the size of the business. In a smaller operation such as the candy distributorship, the owner may choose to perform a couple of reviews, say, the inventory and payroll, while having his accounting supervisor prepare the requirements for the general ledger system. In the case of the ABC Hardware Company, Mr. Jones assigned the inventory requirements definition to his two most experienced store managers. He asked his accounting supervisor to perform the general ledger and accounts payable review while he outlined the requirements for the accounts receivable system.

THE ABC HARDWARE COMPANY

Before beginning the accounts receivable review, Mr. Jones dictated a short memo stating the objective of the review and outlining the steps that were to be followed in developing each of the *system requirements*. Table 6.1 summarizes his memo.

Since the requirements definition process is a natural extension of the needs analysis, Mr. Jones supplied each employee assigned to prepare a requirements document with a copy of the needs analysis document for their respective business functions (Tables 3.1 through 3.5). He also added a note that the requirements document should be simple but well thought out and that special consideration should be given to how the current manual system could be improved both before and after automation.

Mr. Jones' interest in improving the current procedures was the result of his own detailed study of the accounts receivable (A/R) process. During the interview with his accounts receivable clerk he recalled that the A/R statements were prepared only for customers whose balance was in excess of 30 days without any payment. The clerk did not know why customer statements were being prepared in this manner, but observed that very few people paid their bills

TABLE 6.1. A Memo from Bob Jones. Subject: Steps in Developing the Requirements Document

I have asked that each of you review certain aspects of our business in preparation for automation. The following is an outline of the steps you should take. I have also attached the accounts receivable requirements for your consideration. Your objective is to complete the following sentence: "What we really need is a system that will . . ."

Steps to be taken:

1. Get a thorough understanding of the current system by
   a. Sketching the current office paper flow. See the sample I have attached (Figure 6.1. page 65).
   b. Get samples of all documents used in the process.
   c. Note information that is essential to the process.
   d. Document important actions, calculations, and functions.
2. Interview your personnel to
   a. Confirm your sketch.
   b. Identify improvements that could be realized.
3. Prepare a summary of the minimum requirements we need in the system we purchase. See the attached sample (Table 6.2).

Bob Jones

---

prior to receiving a statement. This, the clerk felt, was why 65 percent of ABC's accounts receivable were overdue.

When Mr. Jones established a policy of billing only nonpaying customers, the company was in a different financial position. The first store had just opened and needed customers. To encourage new accounts Mr. Jones announced to his staff that as long as a customer was making a monthly effort to reduce his or her balance, the ABC Hardware store would be satisfied and no past-due statement would be sent. While conducting in-depth interviews for the requirements document, Mr. Jones talked to one store manager who noted that several customers were charging more to their account each month than they were paying. This was increasing the store's accounts receivable and reducing its cash flow.

During the next store managers' meeting Mr. Jones addressed the problem and several suggestions were made which he added to the requirements definition for the accounts receivable system. First, regardless of the age of the balance, the accounts receivable software should produce customer statements on all balances over ten dollars. Second, interest should be charged on all balances over 30 days, and, finally, payments should be applied against the customer's oldest balance. In placing these requirements in his requirements definition, Mr. Jones completed most of the General Processing Section of his requirements document. In the process of developing the requirements he became convinced that detailed interviews, even for employees who already knew the current operation, were an important aspect of defining what the automated system should do.

But there was a second benefit gained during Mr. Jones' study. In his discussions with the bookkeeper, he also discovered that he did not understand how deposits were being made. Bank deposits were being delayed by the accounts receivable posting process. Checks were held for days until they could be posted to the accounts receivable ledgers. Mr. Jones made an immediate change in the company's policy so that the deposit slip became the posting document. He added a place on the deposit slip for the customer's charge account number and saved an extra copy for posting to the accounts receivable ledgers. As a result, checks were deposited daily without affecting the weekly posting of accounts receivable.

This change did not affect the requirements definition but it did result in an immediate improvement in the company's operating efficiency. Operational improvements such as this are a frequent byproduct of the requirements definition process.

CONTENTS OF THE REQUIREMENTS DOCUMENT

Every computer professional has a different concept of what a requirements definition should include. There is no need for formality or even consistency between systems. What is needed is a short, thorough outline of exactly what the software should do for your company. What is important is that the document outline your business requirements in such a manner that a person unfamiliar with your operation could relate your requirements to the computer software available on the market. Experience indicates, however, that there are some basic topics that should be addressed. Among these are the expected transaction volumes of each type of input, special calculations that might be required, and what types of reports are necessary.

In preparing his requirements documents for the accounts receivable system, Mr. Jones addressed six important issues. These are:

1. Input requirements
2. Output and report requirements
3. Calculations and general processing
4. Special requirements
5. Volumes and statistics
6. Special characteristics

For input Mr. Jones indentified two input documents from his current accounts receivable operation that would be necessary during automation. These were the sales ticket and the *sales deposit voucher*. He studied the forms currently in use and identified all the important pieces of information, that is, key "data elements," which were on each form. Those pieces of information that were required to make the current system work properly were denoted by writing "Required" beside the element's name (see Table 6.2).

TABLE **6.2**. Accounts Receivable Requirements Document

INPUT:

1. *Weekly Sales Tickets*
   - Customer number, Required, 4 digits
   - Ticket number, Required, 6 digits
   - Quantity sold
   - Description
   - Department number, Required, 4 digits
   - Store number, Required, 2 digits
   - Dollar amount, Required
   - Date, Required, mm/dd/yy

2. *Weekly Deposit Voucher*
   - Customer number, Required
   - Check number, Required
   - Date of payment, Required
   - Dollar amount, Required
   - Deposit voucher number, Required, 4 digits

Required = required item

TABLE **6.2.** Accounts Receivable Requiresments Document (cont.)

OUTPUT and REPORTS:

1. *Aged Accounts*

Shows a breakdown of the balance of each account by age (30, 60, 90, and over 90 days). Also has total balance, current month balance, and current month payment columns. Should be one line per account and give customer name and account number.

2. *Detailed Account Activity*

Shows balances brought forward from last month plus all activity, including service charges, payments, adjustments, and customer charges.

3. *Stop Credit Report*

Shows customer's full name and address, account number, total balance over 90 days, plus date and amount of last payment. This report should be printed on 8½-by-11-inch paper, which can be bound to eliminate customer exposure at the cash register counter.

4. *Customer Statements*

A customer statement should be printed for each account over $10. Each statement should show all activity on the detailed account activity report plus print year-to-date service charges.

5. *Batch Audit Report*

Gives detail listing of all transactions entered into the system and tests for incorrect account numbers. Also gives total debits and credits for balancing.

6. *Screen Inquiry*

The system should be able to allow a clerk to enter an account number and get a listing on the computer screen of all activity since the last statement.

CALCULATIONS and GENERAL PROCESSING

- Sales tickets and deposit vouchers should be "batched" separately and entered into the computer on a weekly basis.
- Once a month the service charge should be calculated and added to each account.
- The service charge should be calculated at 1.5 percent of the balance over 30 days old.
- All reports should be printed monthly, except the weekly batch audit report.

TABLE **6.2.** Accounts Receivable Requiresments Document (cont.)

SPECIAL REQUIREMENTS
- On a monthly basis a store-level summary of payments and balances should be created and passed to the general ledger system.
- On a monthly basis department-level summaries should be created giving total sales by department within each store. This information should be passed to the inventory system.

VOLUMES and STATISTICS
- 200 sales tickets per month
- 50 payments per month entered on one voucher per week
- 385 charge accounts
- No new stores planned during the next three years
- A growth rate in account and activity of around 20 percent per year

SPECIAL CHARACTERISTICS
- Special use of ABC Hardware letterhead statements.

To be certain that the information was necessary, Mr. Jones drew a rough sketch of how the system worked and marked what information passed through the system and what processing occurred at each step. Figure 6.1 (page 65) is the sketch he drew.

Mr. Jones realized that the accounts receivable system would need to pass information about what was sold to the inventory system. At the same time account balances summarized to the store level are required for the general ledger system. To address these questions he met with the store managers who were performing the other requirement definitions and the bookkeeper. Together they developed a rough plan as to how the *interfaces* between these systems should occur. The information was outlined in the Special Requirements section of each requirements document. In the processing section of the accounts receivable report he noted how each input form had to be handled.

For the output section Mr. Jones identified the reports and information he would require from the software. This included an *aged accounts report*, which would show how long an account balance had been carried. A *detailed activity report* would be required to show all charges and payments during the month for each account, and customer statements would need to be printed

FIGURE 6–1.

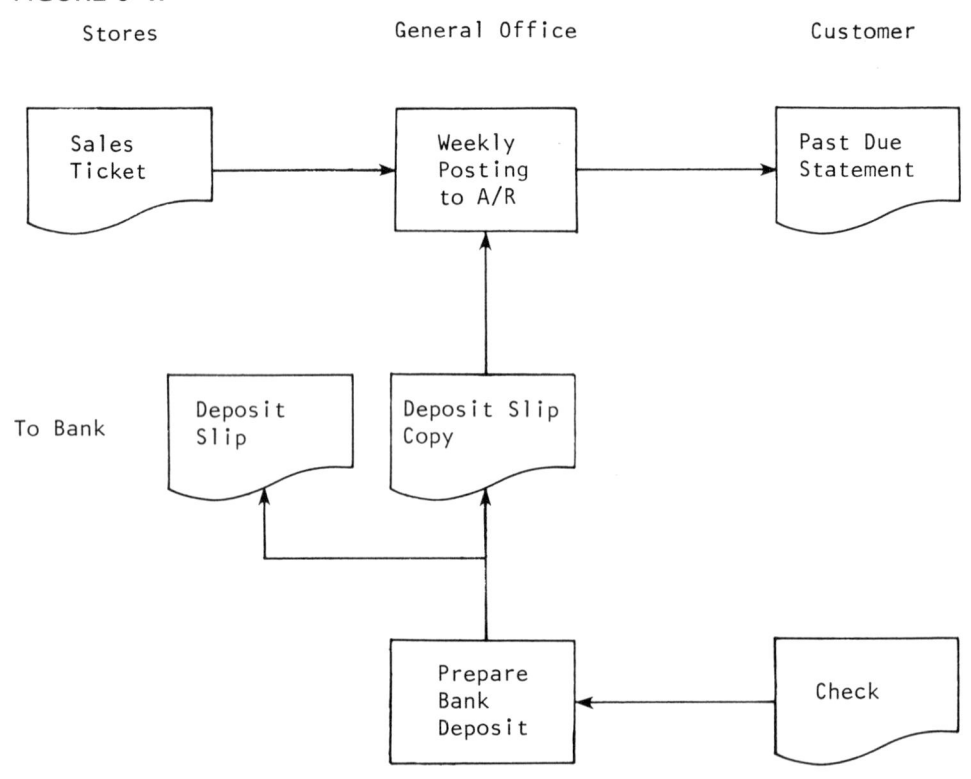

```
         Stores                General Office              Customer

        ┌─────────┐            ┌──────────┐              ┌──────────┐
        │ Sales   │──────────▶ │ Weekly   │ ───────────▶ │ Past Due │
        │ Ticket  │            │ Posting  │              │ Statement│
        └─────────┘            │ to A/R   │              └──────────┘
                               └──────────┘
                                    ▲
                               ┌─────────┐   ┌────────────┐
        To Bank  ◀──────────── │ Deposit │   │Deposit Slip│
                               │ Slip    │   │Copy        │
                               └─────────┘   └────────────┘
                                    ▲              ▲
                                    └──────┬───────┘
                                           │
                                      ┌─────────┐
                                      │ Prepare │         ┌───────┐
                                      │ Bank    │ ◀────── │ Check │
                                      │ Deposit │         └───────┘
                                      └─────────┘
```

showing the same information. Both of these reports should show the monthly service charge, which he determined to be 1.5 percent of the over-30-day balance.

The bookkeeper convinced Mr. Jones that a *past-due customer list*, which showed every account over 90 days old, could be used to halt further charges by delinquent customers. Mr. Jones changed the report title to the *stop-credit report* and added the new report to the output section of the accounts receivable requirements document.

Mr. Jones originally wanted each store to receive a monthly summary report showing each customer's total balance. He called this the *account balance report*. However, during the store managers' meeting it was suggested that this requirement could be met by adding a total balance column to the aged accounts report, thus saving computer time and reducing the amount of paper mailed to each store. It was a good idea and Mr. Jones decided to use it.

Table 6.2 shows how Mr. Jones summarized his findings into a requirements document for the accounts receivable function. This document will be used as an attachment when the vendor letter is written (Chapter 7). But before the letter is prepared a search must occur to find good software vendors. This is the topic of the next chapter.

GLOSSARY

Account Balance Report A report of all balances maintained on an application system, such as accounts receivable as of the report date.

Aged Accounts Report A report showing accounts receivable account balances by customer with a breakdown by age of the amounts due.

Detailed Activity Report A report showing the transactions that have been posted to the master files of an application such as accounts receivable during the current period.

Input Collectively refers to the information that must be input into a computer system in order for the system to operate and maintain the necessary management information.

Interfacing When one software package prepares information in a format that can be used by another package without having to reenter the data through the keyboard.

Output Collectively refers to the reports and screens that are available to the user of a computer system and that allow the user to see the results of calculations and the status of management information.

Past-Due List A report showing those customers who are past due in paying off their accounts receivable balance.

Requirements Definition Statement of the requirements a business has for the performance of a computer system.

Sales Deposit Voucher The document that accompanies a deposit of cash receipts and is the source of posting to the accounts receivable ledger.

Special Characteristics When used in reference to a requirements document this term defines operating characteristics of the desired system. An example would be the need for a printer that can print on standard letter-size paper.

Special Requirements When used in reference to a requirements document, this term designates certain unique characteristics that are desired. An example would be a special report that is needed.

Stop-Credit Report A listing of those customers who have met some predetermined criteria for having their credit cut off.

System Requirements Those characteristics of a system that are necessary for its performance in a particular business environment. See Requirements Definition and Requirements Document.

LOOKING FOR VENDORS

7

Once you have completed the requirements definition document, it is time to begin looking for the stores with the products to fill your needs. The important point at this stage in the acquisition process is to not limit your sources of software. Recently an independent investor who was considering automating her office was approached by a major computer vendor's marketing representative. The salesman explained to the businesswoman all of the advantages of his computer system, arranged a demonstration, and demonstrated a system that fully met the business's needs. The businesswoman was on the verge of buying the system when she read in the newspaper about another small-business computer that was going to be publicly demonstrated at a local hotel. Visiting the demonstration, the investor found an equally acceptable business system but at one-half the cost of the computer she had seen earlier.

Which system should she buy? The answer was that each computer system was designed for a different size of business with different requirements, and the cheaper system fully met her needs. Although cost is certainly not the only consideration, in this case all other factors were equal and cost became a major factor. Only by going through the steps outlined in earlier chapters could the businesswoman make that decision. But she certainly did not want to rule out any alternative vendor sources before checking with them. If she had not seen the second equipment demonstration, she would have purchased the more expensive alternative, which would have met her needs, but at twice the cost.

The best types of software to look for when you begin searching for a computer system are the *canned or packaged programs*. Both terms refer to software that has been written by a vendor for distribution through computer stores, by mail order, or packaged with a hardware system. The advantage gained from taking this approach is that the vendor is able to share his development costs over a wider base. It is the same concept that is used with mass-produced items: increasing the quantity sold reduces the unit cost. Translated, this means that you can buy the programs more cheaply than you could if they were made to meet your specific needs.

There is an obvious disadvantage to adopting the packaged system approach; the software products purchased "off the shelf" lack some of the individual features that are useful to your company. However, we learned in Chapter 1 that manpower costs are the greatest financial factors involved in any computer-system installation. Program design and coding can be extremely labor intensive and thus expensive. A careful balance of cost versus benefit must be evaluated before buying custom software. As a general rule, all attempts at finding an acceptable packaged software system should be exhausted before you consider having custom software developed.

There are many places to shop for computer software products for a small business. The most obvious place is one of the thousands of microcomputer stores that have opened throughout the country. These stores are typically geared toward a wide range of microcomputer users. The result is that shelf space, time, and training are being exhausted on computer hobby and games products at the expense of the small-business systems. Thus, it is easy to be steered toward those products that are within the salesperson's experience or knowledge while passing up other more business-oriented options. Some retail computer stores are taking a small-business system approach and are specializing in small-business software. In such a store you have a greater chance of receiving suggestions from a wider range of software choices. When choosing retail computer stores, first ask what types of software they sell and choose the stores that are most likely to carry the software products you need.

A second source of small-business computers and related software is an office products store. The office products store is a fairly new marketplace for small-business computers, but one that is growing rapidly. Just as typewriters and adding machines were the mainstay of the office of the recent past, so the small-business computer is becoming the necessary tool of the future. Office products store managers have recognized this fact and are adding small-business computers to their offerings. Stores that do not currently make computer systems available will inevitably be forced to do so. Because these stores are carrying a wide range of products besides small-business computers, be wary of promises that are made about system performance and capabilities. The salesperson may be just as new to small-business computers as you are. However, the office products stores do have an advantage in that they are accustomed to dealing with small businesses and understand many of your bookkeeping problems. Also, there is normally an office products store even in a small town. For this reason you do not have to live in a major city to receive individual attention with maintenance problems, ordering supplies, or receiving assistance when you cannot understand your software.

Another alternative in searching for computer software is dealing directly with the software houses that developed the programs or with discount vendors who sell application software at a reduced price. The advantage to this approach is the reduced cost; the disadvantage is that it is more difficult for the small-business owner to locate these companies and to receive services from them. The easiest way to make this contact is to survey a selection of small-business and small-computer magazines and check the ads for software that appears to fit your requirements. Follow up by calling the toll-free number or writing for brochures and the name of the nearest vendor with the product. Finding a place where you can see a software demonstration is important because computer software should never be purchased sight unseen.

A fourth choice in purchasing computer software is to deal with one of the major computer-related manufacturers such as IBM, Xerox, Burroughs, and the like. These companies have sales offices in most major cities and all have small-business lines. In some instances software has been developed within the company. However, the majority of these companies have outside firms write or adapt software for their particular machines. What the hardware vendor then does is prepare a list of available software products and companies to contact for information and demonstrations. The problem with this approach is that you are locked into a hardware decision before you have seen all of the software choices. The advantages are that you can have some level of confidence that your *hardware vendor* will be in business for the life of your computer and that he would not recommend software that is inadequate. Be sure to request a demonstration through the hardware vendor since you can many times see the system in use at a company rather than having only a prepared demonstration.

A final alternative in searching for software products is to ask your accountant or management consultant. Such professionals often deal with small-business systems and can make recommendations based on prior experiences. Your accountant also has the advantage of knowing a great deal about your business. Drawing on this pool of knowledge can give you a more objective recommendation. Even if you choose software from one of the other sources, you may consider having a professional evaluation. Your accountant, after all, will soon be dealing with the effects of your new system, so why not obtain his comments prior to investing.

ABC HARDWARE COMPANY

Mr. Jones began his search for computer products by checking in the business section of his local paper. He found that there were two companies that had advertisements for small-business computers.

One was called Technology Unlimited and the ad featured the Micro-Alpha computer system. The ad also listed various types of software that were available. Among the program products listed in the ad were general ledger, accounts receivable, payroll, and word processing. Bob Jones was not interested in word processing and the ad did not mention inventory software, something he had identified as a definite need. Bob followed the philosophy of not ruling out potential sources until after receiving their responses. As a result, he added Technology Unlimited to his vendor list,

The second source of computer hardware and software that Bob found was Office Products Ltd. This company had a quarter-page advertisement describing office furniture, typewriters, and small-business computers. No software products were listed, but Ring II computer systems were mentioned. Bob was somewhat concerned about the expertise of the company in providing a full range of computer software and hardware products. However, he reasoned that if they specialized in one brand of computers, they would probably be knowledgeable enough to help him. He decided not to eliminate them without first seeing what they had to offer.

Bob continued his search for computer software by checking at his local library for small-business and computer publications. The library carried only a few of the magazines he wanted, but those that they had were full of advertisements for small-business software. He found that the ads seemed to fall into four categories. The first were companies with specialized tax, finance, and modeling software. These ads were very enticing, but Bob realized that he needed to get his core financial accounting functions implemented as stated in his requirements documents before he considered the more sophisticated single-application software. The second type of ad was for word processing. By now Bob had begun to realize that word processing was a very significant market segment and a good potential use for his small-business computer. He made a special note to go back and reconsider word processing as a single-application option for later consideration, but again, only after he had achieved the goals he had set forth in the *requirements documents*.

The third type of ad that Bob encountered was for the fully integrated software company. These ads were for companies that provided general ledger, accounts receivable, accounts payable, and sometimes payroll or inventory software, and all of the program packages interfaced with one another. This was the type of company that Bob was looking for. Unfortunately, none of the companies from this category listed retail inventory software among their offerings.

Bob knew that the companies may have packages that had not been advertised, so he was not deterred. After all, they may know of an inventory package that *interfaced* well with their own software. The final type of ad that Bob encountered was the specialized financial software vendor. These ads listed "improved" and "better" packages of one type or another. Examples included payroll with state tax calculations, inventory with budgeting and order point capabilities, and "enhanced" general ledger. Bob guessed that these were probably new companies breaking into the market. He felt that one way he could use this category of vendor was to send letters to the inventory system suppliers to see if any had a retail inventory system.

To complete his search for a vendor, Bob Jones contacted the major computer vendors in a large city near his home office. He found them listed under "computers" in the phone book. Among other companies listed was Mainframe Computers, Inc. Bob called Mainframe and spoke with one of their account representatives, Evonne Sells. Evonne told Mr. Jones that Mainframe did have a small-business line, the Microframe I and II computers. Ms. Sells indicated that, given his cursory description of his requirements, Mainframe would have the software he needed. Bob took Mainframe's address and told Evonne that he would send a vendor letter to her. In the meantime, Evonne offered to mail Bob a brochure on the Microframe line and to stop by his store for further discussions the next time she was in his town. Bob said that he would like to receive the brochures, but that a visit would be unnecessary until after he had received Mainframe's response to his vendor letter. Satisfied that he had covered all bases, Bob gathered his addresses together and began to think about the vendor letters he would soon be mailing out.

GLOSSARY

Canned or Packaged Programs Computer programs that are written for sale in a mass market to take advantage of economies in spreading the development costs over a wider base.

Hardware Vendor The company that manufactures or assembles the computer hardware that programs are run on.

Interfacing When one software package prepares information in a format that can be used by another package without having to reenter the data through the keyboard.

Program Design and Coding The process of designing, specifying, and writing the logic used by a computer when it performs a programmed task.

Requirements Definition Document Those documents described in Chapter 5 that are the result of defining a business's information-processing requirements.

Small-Business Software Computer programs designed to meet the bookkeeping and management information needs of a small business.

DOCUMENTATION: WHAT TO LOOK FOR

8

If there is a sector of the computer industry that plays a vital role in the success of a system's implementation and yet suffers from the lack of adequate attention, it is documentation. In common terms, documentation is the "owner's manual" for the hardware and software you purchase. There are many facets of documentation depending upon what you are buying. For example, if you purchase a simple computer game you probably will find an *operator's manual*. Of course it won't be called an operator's manual, but as you read it you will find that it tells you how to initiate the programs, which buttons to push, and what instructions to enter to make the system operate properly. There are several types of documentation you will need. Which type depends upon what you are buying (hardware versus software) and what is included in the price (*machine code* versus *machine code* and *source code*). Regardless of what you purchase, it is important that you understand each of the major types of documentation and where they might apply to your needs.

USER DOCUMENTATION

If you are buying a sophisticated software package, you should expect to get considerably more documentation than if you are buying a simple package. *User documentation,* for example, should be provided to inform and train the *end user* on how to fill out any special forms the system requires, how to tell the software to perform certain calculations and functions, and how to request special *on-request reports*. On most large computer systems user documentation gets less attention and less time committed to it than any other documentation group. In many cases the user is left on his own to develop the documentation necessary to make the software function for him. Of course in your case this is impossible since you don't understand how the system operates. Be careful to closely evaluate the user documentation that is included in the purchase price. Unfortunately the vendor will rarely refer to user documentation or user manuals. In that case look carefully for documentation that explains to the user exactly what he can expect from the system and how he can get it.

SYSTEMS DOCUMENTATION

When, as part of the purchase price, you receive *source code,* that is, the programs themselves, then you should also expect to receive two other forms of documentation. The first is the *systems documentation,* which describes how the entire system works from a programmer's point of view. This documentation section should give a high-level, functional description of what each group of programs does within the system. For example, for an accounts receivable package there will be a series of programs that is used to update a customer's background data. This might typically include three programs—one to change the customer's name and address, one to change his balance due for the over-30, over-60, over-90, and current-balance fields, and perhaps a third to change the credit ratings.

The systems documentation should first present an overall picture of the system. This can be done through narrative, high-level flowcharts, sample output reports, and the like. Following the general or high-level description, the systems documentation should break each functional part of the software into subsections or modules that are more or less functionally independent. An example might be an accounts receivable package that has an input and edit function, a calculations and posting function, and a reporting function. Following this level of documentation there should be a further refinement, or at least more detail on how each function is further broken down into subfunctions. Eventually specific programs are identified. Usually this is where the systems documentation will end.

The concept of presenting the system in increasingly more detailed language is called leveling, or stair stepping, the documentation. Figures 8.1 through 8.3 show a typical accounts receivable functional flowchart at three levels. Figure 8.1 is the highest-level chart, followed by 8.2, which explains the input and editing function at a more detailed level. Figure 8.3 then presents the "enter new customer" portion of the input and editing function to the level of the programs themselves. Note that as you work your way down through the levels of documentation more and more details are presented about how the information itself is passed through the system. This level of detail is not important to you specifically, but if your people are to make changes to the system then this level of detail will be invaluable. This is particularly useful if the programmer is inexperienced or is a contract programmer who is not familiar with the package you purchased.

FIGURE 8–1. Special Forms

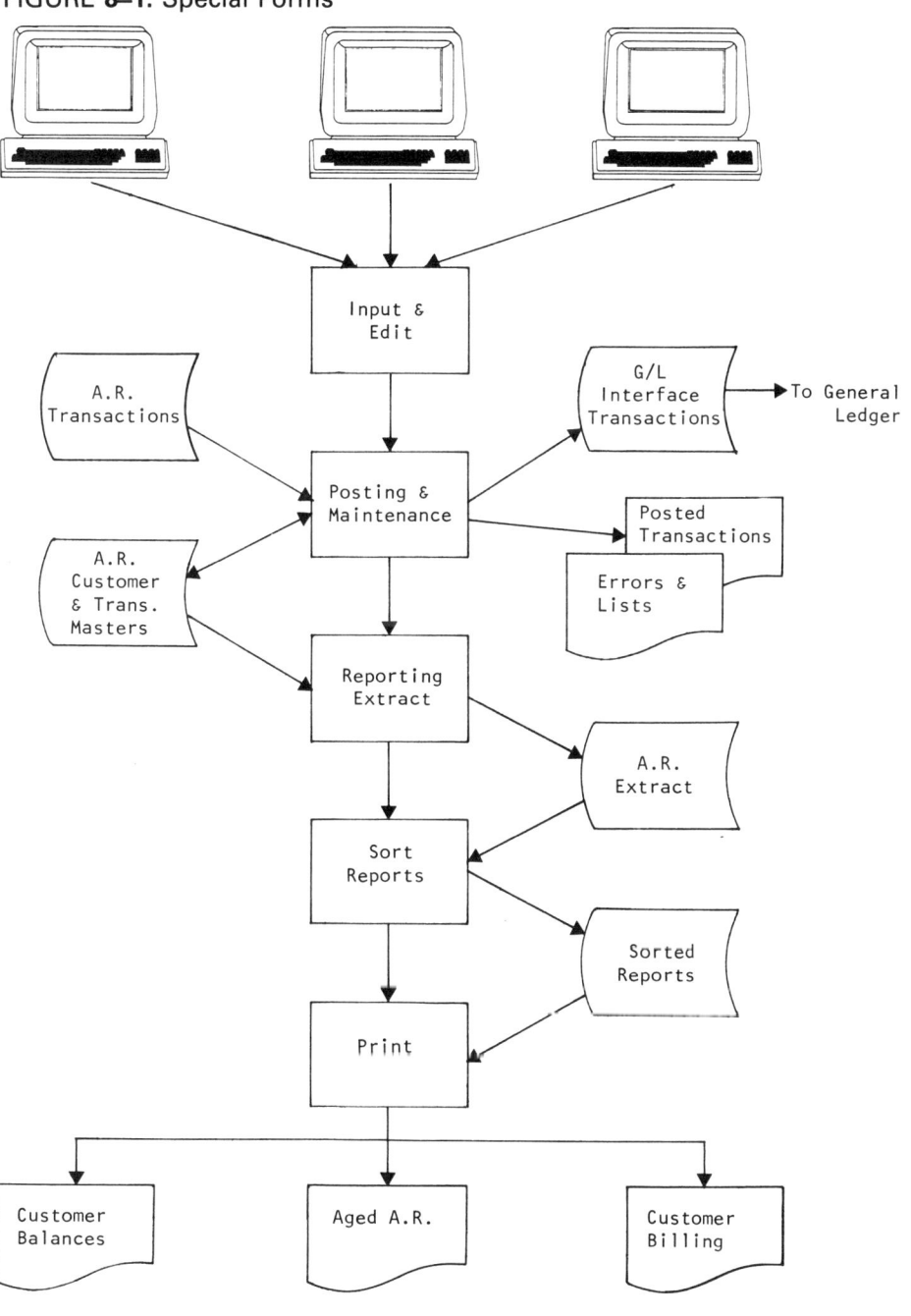

FIGURE 8-2. Post and Maintenance Function

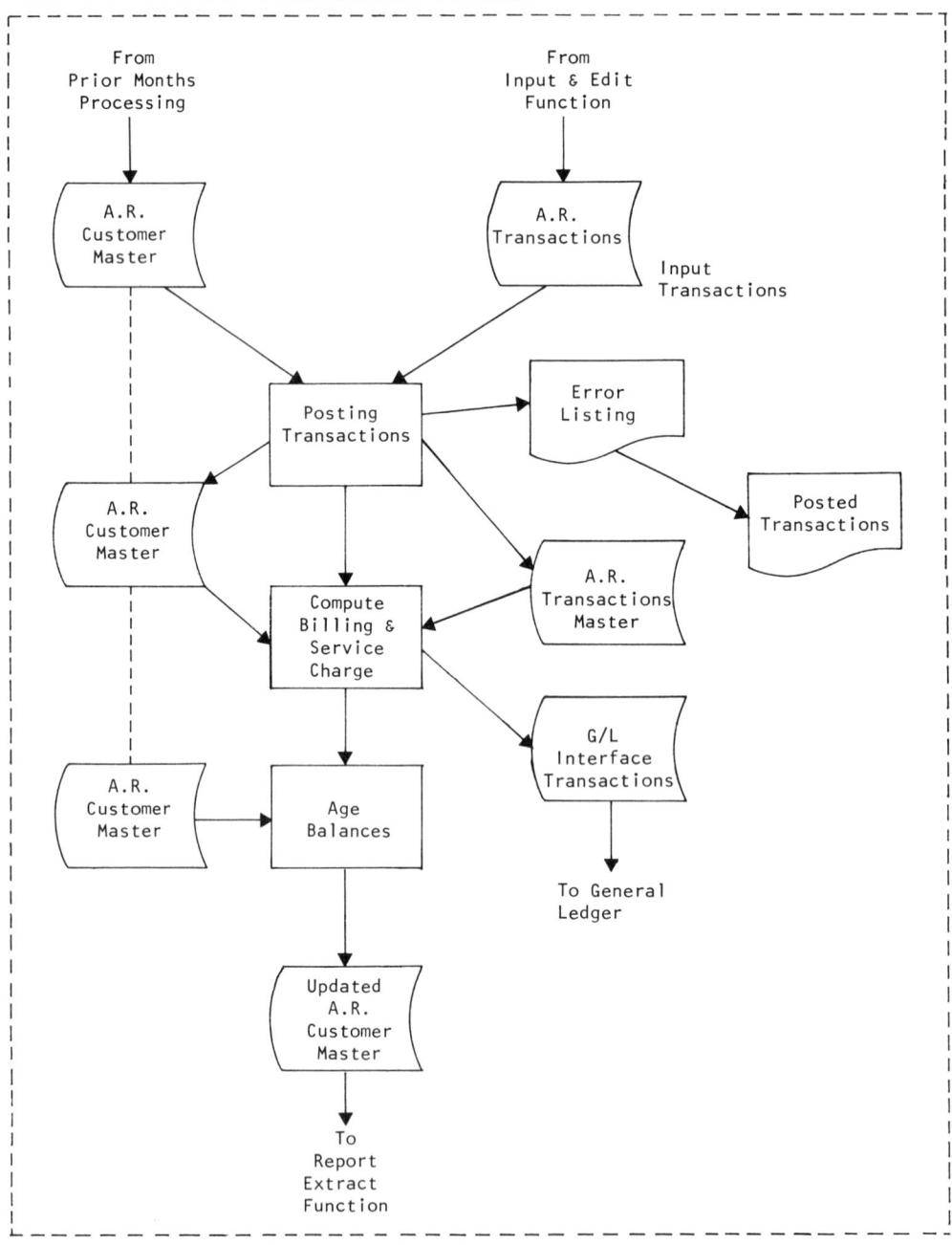

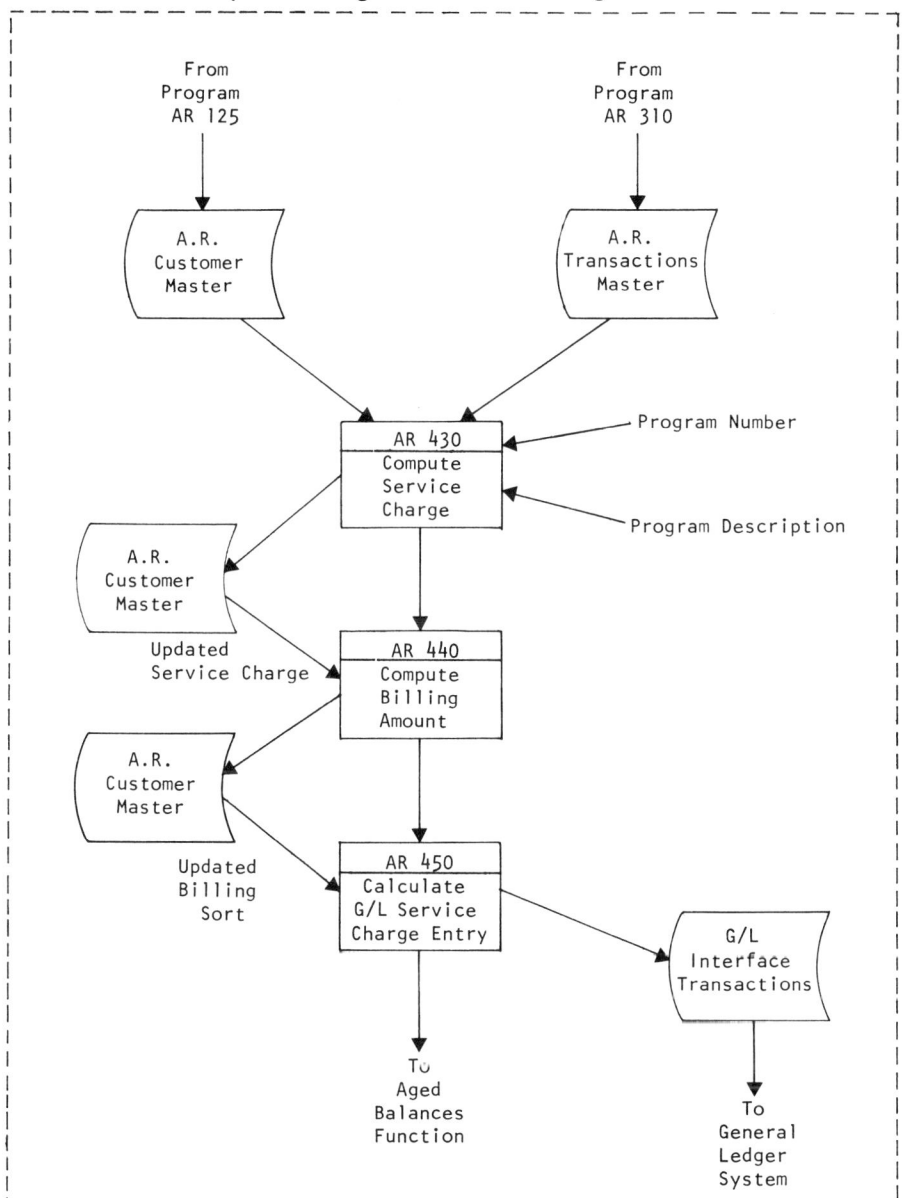

FIGURE 8-3. Compute Billing and Service Charge Subfunction

Of course, the *leveled approach to documentation* is not always used. In fact, since documentation is sometimes ignored or minimized, the leveled approach should be viewed as the ideal. Leveled documentation is not what is important. The important factor is that the systems documentation be present in some form and that it present a high-level overview and a detailed program-level presentation of the system. When you have to modify the programs, anything less will not be adequate.

PROGRAM DOCUMENTATION

The second form of documentation that you should expect when you receive the source code is the *program documentation*. This set of documentation carries the concept of leveling one step further. For every program identified in the detailed systems flowchart (Figure 8.3) there should be a self-contained set of documentation about that program. You are now dealing with the programmer's level of documentation and it is not necessary that you understand what is being presented. It is, however, important that a programmer be able to understand exactly how each program works and what the program is doing. If you have a programmer on staff or you know who will be maintaining the programs for you, have that person review the program documentation before you buy. In particular, have that person look for the following important items:

1. Program Specifications

    A detail description of the general logic within each program. This is the most desirable piece of documentation, but is also the one you will be least likely to find.

2. Sample Report and Screen Formats

    As shown in Figure 8.4, the screen layouts show what the user will actually see when using the system. You should also expect to find sample reports of every document printed by the system. Both sample reports and screen formats are necessary for adequate documentation.

3. Comment Statements

    Have your programmer/analyst look at the program's source code and see that comments are imbedded in the code that explain what function each portion of the program is performing.

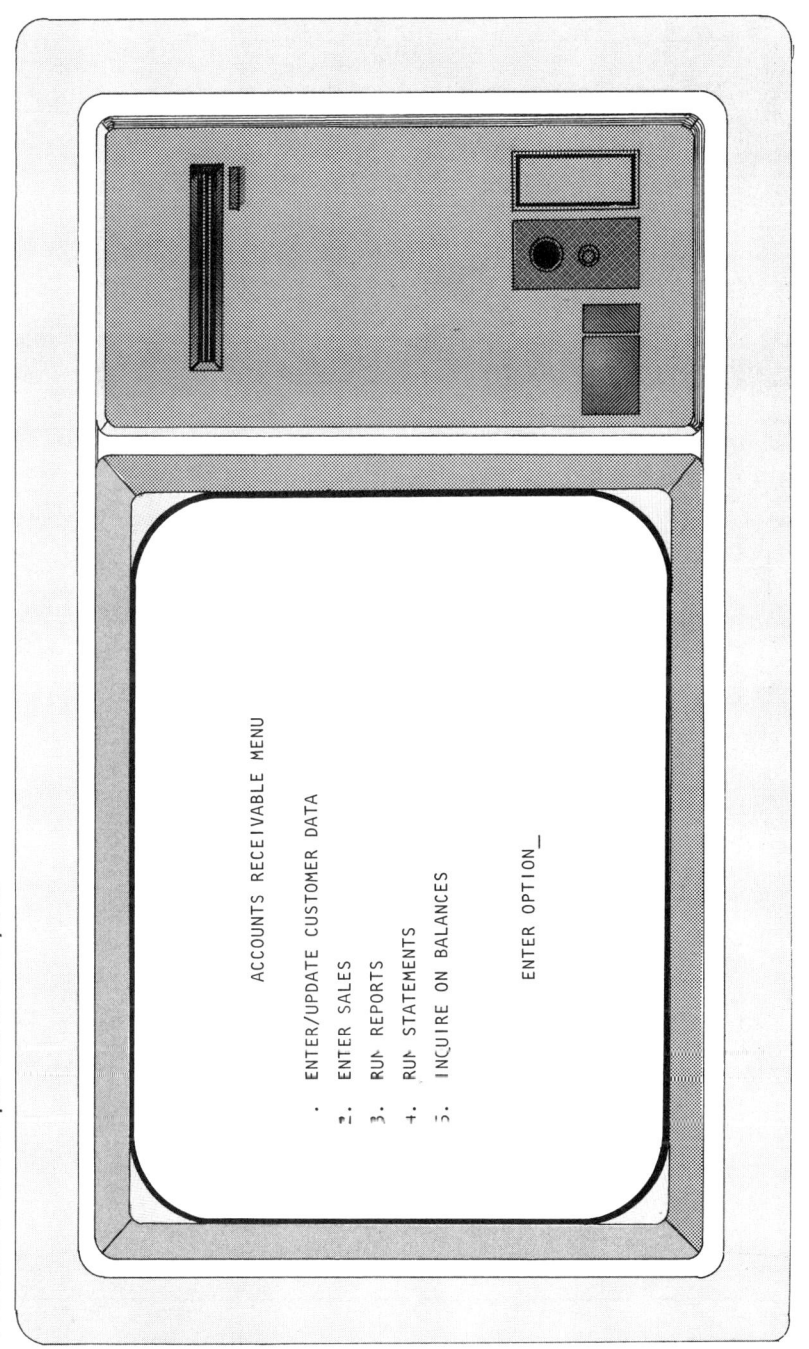

FIGURE 8-4. Sample Screen Layout

```
        ACCOUNTS RECEIVABLE MENU

     1. ENTER/UPDATE CUSTOMER DATA
     2. ENTER SALES
     3. RUN REPORTS
     4. RUN STATEMENTS
     5. INQUIRE ON BALANCES

               ENTER OPTION___
```

FIGURE 8-5. Record Layout

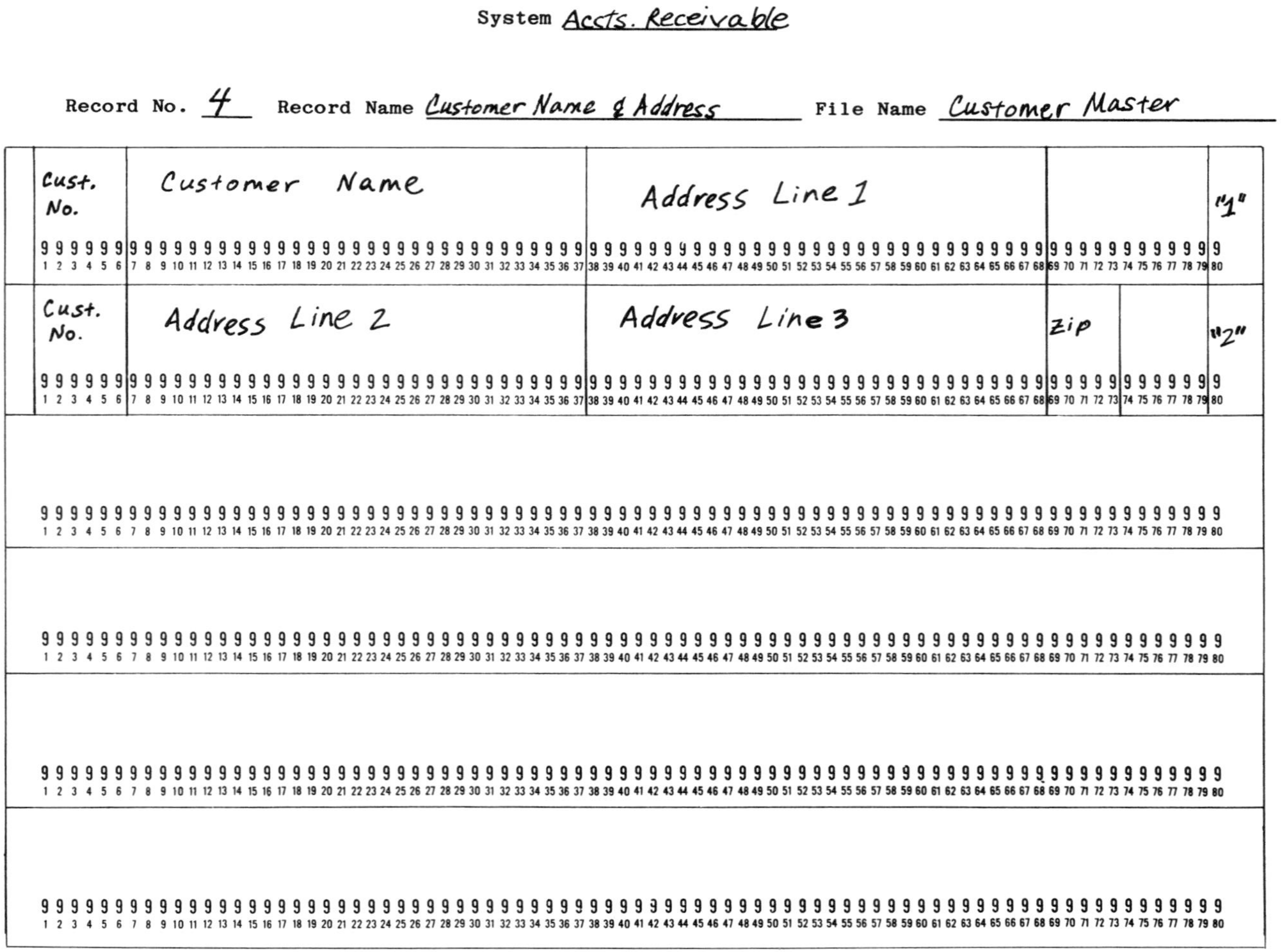

System _Accts. Receivable_   Record No. _4_   Record Name _Customer Name & Address_   File Name _Customer Master_

Cust. No. (1-5)	Customer Name (6-37)	Address Line 1 (38-69)	(70-79) "1" (80)
Cust. No. (1-5)	Address Line 2 (6-37)	Address Line 3 (38-69)	Zip (70-74) (75-79) "2" (80)

4. File and Record Layouts
> Detailed descriptions of what information is stored on peripheral devices and where in the various files the information is stored. See Figure 8.5 for a record layout prepared by ABC Hardware.

If the program documentation has at least these four items then it's probably well documented. Again, you don't have to understand the program documentation itself—that's your programmer's job. Keep in mind, though, that your maintenance costs in modifying the programs will be in direct relationship to the quality of the systems documentation and program documentation. Many program changes require the programmer to spend two thirds of his time trying to figure out what the program does before he can make the change itself. Good documentation is a money maker, particularly in the area of systems and programming documentation.

Many software vendors do not sell the source programs with the system. What this also means is that you cannot modify the programs. Naturally this means the vendor must make the changes, and of course they'll have a monopoly on pricing. This is not necessarily bad, if before you buy you recognize the possibility and negotiate the cost per hour for future changes. If the programmers who developed the system work for the vendor then this could be a big plus for you. No one knows the programming details better than the people who wrote the programs. But don't always assume that the vendor developed the system. Many times they simply own the rights to market the software and the programmers who wrote the software do not work for them. That can be a big problem. Be sure to ask the vendor about program maintenance. If it will be your responsibility then expect systems and program documentation.

OPERATIONS DOCUMENTATION

User, systems, and programming documentation pertain primarily to the purchase of software. This is because they deal with what the software does (systems), how to maintain it (programming), and how to use it (user). You will rarely find these three included when you buy hardware. However, there is one set of documentation that is important both in hardware purchases and software purchases. This documentation is the *operator's manual*. When you buy any piece of computer equipment you should receive some form of operation's documentation (the owner's manual mentioned earlier). The operator's manual should explain how to turn on the equipment, how to make it function, what types of problems might occur and what to do for each, and how to tell the equipment what to do. This is key information and all new computers purchased from the vendor will have it. If you're considering used equipment be sure it includes the operations documentation manual.

Like hardware, software packages should have the same basic type of operations manuals. The software operator's manual should instruct the computer operator on how to operate the software on the particular computer being used. The operator's manual is to the computer operator what the user's manual mentioned earlier is to the end user.

THE CASE-STUDY WALKTHROUGH APPROACH

When small-business computers first became popular the manufacturers were struggling with the question of how to document their products. At first there was very little documentation and it was poorly done. This tendency followed the trends of most large systems developers at that time. In recent years improved documentation has become a goal of large- and small-systems developers alike. With the exploding market for minis and micros, the small-business computer industry has found itself addressing a whole new realm of users: hobbyists, educators, and businesspeople. None of these users are technical data processing people, and as a result the need for effective, user-friendly documentation has become enormous. Currently the best approach is the "Case-Study Walkthrough" approach. Documentation written in this manner will begin by walking the reader through the startup procedure and then will step by step take the reader through one or more sample uses of the system. In this manner the reader, regardless of his prior knowledge, will learn how to initiate and use the system. More complicated, technical subjects are then covered in the later chapters where the reader has already had some *hands-on* experience with the system. For both hardware and software documentation, the case-study walkthrough approach has been the most effective way to present the user and operational documentation, and at the same time train the user on the use of the system.

WHAT TO LOOK FOR IN DOCUMENTATION

Documentation manuals should be written for the people who have to use them and not for the people who wrote them. A quick review of each manual will indicate who the intended reader is. When considering the purchase of a computer or a software package there are five questions you should ask yourself about the documentation.

1. What Level of Knowledge Is Assumed?

Good documentation assumes no prior knowledge of the subject, while adequate documentation assumes only basic knowledge. If the manuals read like a college physics or chemistry book then they are not even adequate. Even the most technical of all the types of documentation should not overwhelm you or appear foreign. The other manuals should read as if they were written for both you and your staff, not your accountant and your staff programmer. When you scan the documentation read a couple of pages closely to determine the level of knowledge assumed.

2. How Well Are the Manuals Organized?

Scan through the manuals without reading them. Can you understand the topics and the organization from the headings? Are subheadings used effectively? Can you easily find a topic without looking for the index or reading every page?

Small-business systems will often have the entire set of documentation in only one or two manuals. This is acceptable as long as you can find what you need quickly. It should not take more than a minute to locate an error code or the systems overview narrative. If there are only one or two manuals that came with the system, then how well they are organized can become an important factor.

3. Are There Illustrations, Examples, and Case Studies?

A picture is worth a thousand words, and a few good illustrations can reduce the size of the documentation by considerable factors.

87

Examples are excellent tools for making a point and they should be used extensively. As you page through the manuals check the pictures, samples, and illustrations closely. Are they well done? Do they say a lot?

4. Do the Manuals Contain Error-Code Tables?

Using error-code tables is an effective way for a computer program to tell the user what is wrong without having to go into great detail within the program itself. The idea is for the program to display a code that the user can look up in an error-code table where detailed information is provided about what caused the error and what the operator or user can do to recover. If this concept is to be used effectively the documentation manuals must provide a useful and meaningful error-code table. Check the back of the manuals where the error-code tables are usually kept. There should be only one table per manual, not several. Check a few of the codes. Are the narratives descriptive of what happened? Are your options for recovery clear? Do they detail what actions can or should be taken? Are the codes organized so that finding the code is easy? Check the error-code tables closely. It is your roadmap to recovering from errors and system problems.

5. Does the Documentation Use the Case-Study Walkthrough Approach?

The case-study walkthrough approach has been very successful in training nontechnical employees how to use small-business systems. Check the documentation and count it a plus if this approach is used in the manuals.

SUMMARY

Before you buy, evaluate the quality and appropriateness of the manuals included in the purchase agreement. If your purchase includes hardware equipment, there should be an operator's manual. If the case-study walkthrough approach is used these may be combined into one manual. If you are also buying the systems source code then both the systems documentation manuals and the program documentation manuals should be included. Without this documentation the source code is almost useless to you.

When you evaluate the vendor's proposals be sure to include the documentation that will be supplied and apply an evaluations weighting factor of not less than 10 percent; 20 percent is more common, but in general is considered to be the maximum weighting factor for documentation. The subject of evaluating the vendor's response is covered in Chapter 10. When you perform this evaluation, do not underestimate the importance of documentation. Documentation will be a key factor in your overall level of satisfaction once the system is operational.

GLOSSARY

End Users The individuals who are to receive the final product (printed reports, displayed results, and so on) from the system.

Error-Code Table A table or glossary of all the errors that a program or system may encounter. Usually a short mnemonic code, such as PE02 (programmer error number 2), is given, followed by a detailed description of the error condition. The mnemonic codes are listed in alphabetical order for easy access.

Hands On A term that refers to a person's having access for operating the hardware equipment.

Leveled Approach to Documentation An approach to documentation in which a high-level overview is given, followed a more detailed description, followed by still another more descriptive narrative, until the most detailed level of documentation is reached. With complex systems each level is generally subdivided to simplify the more detailed descriptions.

Machine Code The computer-readable instructions that are the result of the computer's "reading" (compiling) a computer program. See *Machine-Oriented Computer Language, High-Level Language, Low-Level Language*.

On-Request reports Reports from a computer system that can be printed upon the user's request. Often these reports are not printed unless the user requests them.

Operator's Manual Operations documentation that tells the computer operator how to operate the system and describes the system functions performed.

Program Documentation The set of documentation that describes the interworkings of all programs in a software package.

Source Code The English-like computer instructions that make up a computer program. See *High-Level Language* and *Low-Level Language*.

Systems Documentation The set of documentation that gives a complete overview of the software system. The systems documentation generally includes flowcharts showing how data flows from program to program and how the various subfunctions are related.

User's Documentation The documentation that explains to the end user what the system can do for each user and how to prepare input and instructions so the system will perform the proper functions. See *End User*.

HOW TO WRITE A VENDOR LETTER

9

Once you have completed your vendor list, it is time to take the plunge and send out vendor letters. You have as much information as you can gain given your level of computer skills, so it is now necessary to rely on others. The letters ask the vendors to propose solutions to your data processing needs. You must carefully decide on the right moment to send your vendor letter. Too much time spent in the vendor list preparation is time lost without a decision. On the other hand, a quick decision is often regretted later in time, satisfaction, and money lost.

The vendor letter, also known as a *request for proposal* (RFP), is a formal way of requesting price quotations. It is intended to communicate all information necessary for a response to be made, the format for preparation, and the methods that will be used in evaluating responses. The letter must be concise, appropriate for your vendor's needs, and well written. Otherwise you will find yourself with few choices when the time to make a selection arrives. A good vendor letter saves legwork in gathering facts, provides a means of fairly evaluating competitive packages, and leaves the small-business owner with a structured approach to making his or her system selections.

There are several sections to a vendor letter. The general categories include the cover letter, the general information section, and the requirements section. The cover letter should be addressed to the contact person as taken from the vendor list. As was noted earlier, this may be different from the person who gave the initial demonstration. Next, the letter should overview the types of software being sought. You are saving the detailed points for the later sections and you should refer to what material may be found there. Finally, leave the possibility open for further contact by stating that questions should be directed to you.

The body of the vendor letter should contain the following two main sections with the delineated subsections:

1. General Information Section
    - Background material on company
    - Software requested
    - Deadline for responses
    - Response format
    - Timetable and methods for evaluating responses

2. Requirements Section
   - General requirements
   - Volumes estimated and other points
   - Special hardware requirements
   - Available documentation
   - Maintenance availability and costs
   - Proposed conversion assistance

The information contained in these subsections may be seen in the following paragraphs and in the case study that follows this chapter.

The background material must tell the prospective suppliers enough about your company to enable them to understand your business environment. The description need not be exhaustive. It will be hard to determine what factors are necessary for a vendor to know, so only hit the high points. You have already invited the suppliers to inquire if they have further questions, so let them decide what you have left out. Along with this concept of background material goes the idea of a software requested section. As you can see from the outline, this information will be covered in much more detail later. The background material subsection is an overview. It summarizes in broad terms what this letter is requesting.

The next two subsections of the vendor letter specify the deadline and format for responses. The first part, the deadline, is necessary both for you and for the vendor. You do not want to wait long for responses and you also do not want to spend your valuable time phoning vendors to request their responses. Similarly, it is important for the vendor to understand the time frame in which he is working. A definite schedule for responses is more likely to be answered promptly than is a request that is vague in its time requirements. The format subsection serves both you and the vendor. The evaluation is much easier if all responses have similar formats. This eliminates your having to glean evaluative information from the body of the response. Also, the vendor can better respond when he understands what is being requested.

The timetable and methods for evaluating responses section gives specific information on what the vendor can expect. Again, detailing this information in the beginning clarifies your thoughts and lets the vendor know that you are a serious customer. Request that the vendor not contact you concerning your decision prior to the date of decision. You do not want a continuous stream of phone calls with vendors asking for your decision. Also, when a persistent salesperson who wants to know your decision does call, you now have something to refer him to: a date when you will get back to him. Do not be too concerned about developing a detailed evaluation plan. A short list of the points you consider important and the weights attached to each is more than adequate. Anything more complicated is likely to be cumbersome and inappropriate for the costs involved.

You have now completed a one-page cover letter and a one- to one-and-a-half-page general information section. The last part of the vendor letter is the requirements section, the subsections of which are taken from the requirements document you completed in Chapter 6. In fact, if your requirements document is well formatted, you may send it as is in place of this section. If you decide to take this approach, make sure that all of the points noted below are present in your requirements document.

The first two subsections are old friends. One is the software requirements subsection, which contains the major points from your requirements document. The second subsection contains the volume estimates and other minor points as taken from the needs analysis and requirements definition. It is now time to get down to some of the specific questions you have been avoiding. No system will meet all of your needs, but the closest fit will probably be the system selected.

The next two subsections detail special hardware requirements and available documentation. The first is used when there are specific hardware needs that the vendor must address in his proposal. Examples would be to identify requirements for *point of sale equipment*, multicolor printers, or terminals away from the main site. The second subsection covers available *documentation*, that is, what books, manuals, and forms are provided to explain how the software works. An example of the type of computer language to use can be seen in the case study that follows. The importance of this request is attested to by a buyer who did not receive adequate documentation. There is no feeling more helpless or frustrating than that felt by someone who is in the middle of a computer run when the procedures manual fails to detail the next step.

The final two subsections of the requirements section ask for information about maintenance and conversion assistance. Both are fairly straightforward and are shown in the case study following. The maintenance subsection requests information concerning repair facilities. Micro- and minicomputers and peripherals often break down. You should not be surprised to find that your microcomputer printer will break down twice a year if it is used heavily. With checks waiting to be printed, you don't want to wait a month while the printer flies cross-country. Similarly, the conversion assistance subsection asks for the vendor's plan for, and intended assistance with, getting your system up and running. What is needed is a vendor who is ready and available to help when you hit that inevitable first snag.

BOB JONES' VENDOR LETTER— A CASE STUDY

Using the vendor list that he prepared in Chapter 7, Bob Jones prepared his vendor letter. He selected Wright Office Products, XYZ Business Computers, and Mainframe Computers to send the requests to, since they represented the most likely sources of software as indicated on the vendor list. Bob followed the suggested format in writing his letters and prepared a standard general information section. Because of the time he had spent on the requirements document, Bob chose to add a few points concerning maintenance availability and proposed conversion assistance, and then used the requirements document as the requirements section. He then tailored the three cover letters to the types of vendors with whom he was dealing. Following is one of the cover letters and the general information sections as he prepared them.

GENERAL INFORMATION SECTION

A. *Background*—ABC Hardware Co. is a retail dealer in hardware items. ABC's main store is located in Anytown, Texas and has two other stores in Suburb and Smalltown. ABC Hardware Co. has maintained its sales and inventory on a manual basis since its inception.

B. *Software Requested*—ABC Hardware Co. is requesting that submitted proposals contain the following software:

- General ledger
- Accounts receivable
- Accounts payable
- Inventory

C. *Deadline for Responses*—Responses must be received by Aug. 1 to be considered.

12 September 1983

Mr. Howard Banks
Account Representative
XYZ Business Computers
Anytown, Texas 77777

Dear Mr. Banks:

I am writing you concerning our conversation of last week in which we discussed the general ledger, accounts payable, accounts receivable, and inventory systems which ABC Hardware Co. is currently seeking. We are asking vendors to submit proposed software and hardware systems that fit our needs. The attached sheets contain information concerning background, deadlines, formats, evaluation processes, and requirements.

If you have any questions concerning these specifications, do not hesitate to call me. I look forward to receiving your response.

Sincerely,

Robert R. Jones
President
ABC Hardware Co.

D. *Response Formats*—Responses should include at least one page of detail for each application proposed and a summary page covering how the applications interface with each other.

E. *Timetable and Methods for Evaluating Responses*—Proposals will be evaluated and successful candidates notified by Aug. 15. The weighting of proposals will be as follows:

    40%—Meets requirements
    25%—Cost
    15%—Documentation
    10%—Maintenance availability
    10%—Conversion assistance

GLOSSARY

Computer Languages Languages that people can use to tell the computer what to do. Languages can be high-level (English-like) or low-level (closer to the computer's natural language). See *Low-Level Language* and *High-Level Language*.

Documentation The collection of documents that provides information to the users of a computer system. The varieties of documentation typically found include maintenance, operating, and user.

Point of Sale Equipment Equipment used to receive sales information at the time it occurs (e.g. at the cash register). This is in contrast to waiting until the end of the day to enter sales information using accumulated sales slips or other documents.

Request for Proposal A document generally consisting of a vendor letter and requirements documents which is sent to vendors to request that they prepare a proposal to meet the customer's needs. See *Vendor Letter* and *Requirements Document*.

EVALUATING VENDOR RESPONSES

10

The evaluation of the vendor's responses is a simple three-step process. The first step, preparation, involves preparing an evaluation work sheet, reviewing each proposal as it arrives, and separating the responses into the various applications. Stage two is to evaluate the responses by application and to identify which of the proposed systems meet the application's requirements. The final step involves summarizing the lists of acceptable proposals by vendor in preparation for the demonstrations that will be requested next (Chapter 11). It should be pointed out that the objective of the vendor-evaluation process is not to pick the best system but rather to determine which of the proposed systems meet the various application requirements as they are outlined in your requirements document. The final decision concerning the best system for your company will be made after the demonstrations have been performed.

THE PREPARATION PHASE

Although the actual evaluation process cannot begin until after the response deadline that was established in your vendor letter, some preparation can begin as the responses arrive. It is not necessary, for example, to wait until the deadline before opening the responses. The objective is to perform a preliminary review to verify that the response is a *proposal* and not a *letter of inquiry*. Often the vendor may write for clarification about some point in the requirements document. If the response is a letter requesting clarification, then your response should be prepared immediately. Prompt, straightforward, and honest answers will allow the vendor to finalize and mail his proposal in time to meet your deadline.

It is not uncommon for a vendor to question the accuracy of your requirements documents. This is not the time to reconsider your requirements. If you lack confidence in your needs analysis or requirements documents then seek outside advice before you mail the vendor letter. Most vendors are honest and helpful. However, to get a truly unbiased opinion it is best to recruit your accountant or a local consulting firm with demonstrated small-business and data processing skills. Such a person could review your requirements document and help prepare your vendor letter. In either case don't rewrite your requirements after they have been mailed to vendors.

As you open the vendors' responses, weed out the proposals from query letters and set the proposal letters aside until the deadline stated in your vendor letter. Frequently a vendor who was not on your original list may respond with a proposal. Consider this to be a good sign. Obviously your vendor letter is the talk of the town. Take advantage of the opportunity by adding the new vendor to your vendor list and placing the unsolicited proposal in your stack of vendor responses. It may be just the proposal you want.

While you're waiting for the proposal deadline, take some time to prepare an evaluation sheet such as the one shown in Figure 10.1. There should be one sheet for each application being considered. Figure 10.1 is the evaluation sheet prepared by Bob Jones for ABC Hardware's accounts receivable application. The factors and weights used to evaluate each proposed system should be identical to those outlined in your vendor letter. However, if the requirements document noted several "special requirements," then the "meets requirements" column of the evaluation sheet may need to be subdivided into two or more columns. The division will allow each special consideration to be evaluated separately. It is important not to divide the evaluated columns unless the subcategories justify special consideration. If you do divide the categories, be sure that the total evaluation weights for all the subcategories equal the total weight allocated in the vendor letter. Otherwise you will be applying more (or less) importance to this category than you said you would in the vendor letter.

For example, Mr. Jones subdivided his "meets needs" category on the accounts receivable evaluation sheet into two subcategories; 1. meets general needs, and 2. meets special needs. He gave weights of 30 and 10, respectively, which total the 40 points he allocated to the "meets needs" category in his vendor letter. When the evaluation work sheet is prepared, all the vendor inquiries have been answered, and the response deadline has passed, then the actual evaluation process can begin.

THE EVALUATION PHASE

A few days after the deadline given in your vendor letter, the process of evaluating the vendor proposals should begin. Don't be surprised by the mixture of responses. Some responses may be well-prepared proposals that respond to each item on the requirements document. Others may have a one-page letter stating which applications the vendor has and at what cost. Many retail outlets use a cover letter

FIGURE 10-1. ABC Hardware

VENDOR EVALUATION SHEET
ACCOUNTS RECEIVABLE

| Vendor | Cost Range | Meets Needs | | Cost | Maint. Ability | Conversion Assist. | Documen- tation | Total Points | PROs & CONs |
		General	Special						Comments
Weights		30	10	25	10	10	15	100	

103

followed by copied materials from the documentation or sales material for each system. This type of response often gives more information but requires you to decipher the information and fit it to your requirements document.

In either case the first step is to study each vendor's proposal as a whole. That is, read the entire proposal regardless of the number of applications and try to gain an understanding of what the vendor is proposing. Make notes of your reactions, good and bad, as you study the proposal. When you have a good feel for what is being proposed, separate the proposals into the various systems being reviewed. The next step will be to evaluate all the payroll systems together, then move to accounts receivable, payroll, and so on. Use your requirements document for your guideline and the *vendor evaluation sheet* to grade each proposed system.

Although it is often difficult to divide a proposal into its various applications, this separation should be done so that the various vendor responses can be evaluated on similar grounds. All accounts receivable systems should be evaluated on the same basis. The same is true for each application you have included in your *request for proposal* (RFP). The objective at this stage is to identify which proposed systems in each application will meet your requirements, not which proposal best fits your requirements. You may have six responses for a general ledger system but perhaps only three actually fit your needs. Don't worry about intermixing the same vendor's various proposed applications. You still have your notes from the initial review where you considered each response as a whole.

Even though it may be best to buy most of the applications from one vendor, you don't want to buy any application from a vendor that does not meet your requirements. After all the proposals have been studied they will be regrouped by vendor, so concentrate right now on whether the applications meet your requirements.

For each application, evaluate the proposals independently and rate the system's ability to meet your needs in each of the categories on the evaluation sheet. If the vendor did not address one of the categories then a call may be necessary. Keep in mind, however, that the number of calls required to evaluate a proposal is a fair indication of how well prepared the proposal was. Of course it is best to collect all your questions until you have finished the review. Figure 10.2 shows the results of Mr. Jones' evaluation of the accounts receivable systems. During this process Bob called two vendors to gain a better understanding of their proposals. In particular he couldn't understand the pricing scheme of Quick Systems Inc.

FIGURE 10-2. ABC Hardware

VENDOR EVALUATION SHEET
ACCOUNTS RECEIVABLE

Vendor	Cost Range	Meets Needs General	Meets Needs Special	Cost	Maint. Ability	Conversion Assist.	Documen- tation	Total Points	PROs & CONs Comments
Weights		30	10	25	10	10	15	100	
Quick System	24,200	30	5	20	10	10	15	90	Very nice system. Good salesman.
Mainframe Computers	14,250	10	0	25	0	0	5	40	Low cost but not acceptable software.
Improved Paper Products	25,070	30	10	20	10	10	10	90	Software looks good! People are aggressive and interested!
National Software	20,050	30	5	25	10	5	5	80	Over all good.
Quality Systems	31,255	25	5	15	10	10	10	75	Good software but salesman doesn't know his system.
Every System Inc.	18,175	25	5	25	0	5	15	75	Good documentation but no maintenance help!

Quick Systems had added a charge for each option included in the package. In his telephone conversation with the vendor, Bob decided to consider the system with all the options, thus simplifying the cost.

After completing his evaluation, Bob rated the responses based upon a number of total points. As Figure 10.2 shows, there were five highly rated responses. Mr. Jones decided that any of the five systems would meet his needs. Therefore, Quick Systems, Improved Paper Products, National Software, Quality Systems, and Every System Inc. were all chosen for the demonstration visit.

At this point Bob felt good about his candidates. He knew all five would do the job and he looked forward to seeing each system demonstrated.

RECOGNIZING AN EDSEL

With all the advertising and promotion that preceded the Edsel, when it finally appeared in the showrooms everyone recognized it. Unfortunately for the manufacturer no one wanted to buy one. So it will be with your vendor responses. Don't worry about not recognizing a bad proposal; you will know one when you see it. Probably the first thing you will notice is that it is handwritten or poorly typed on onionskin paper or some other cheap grade of paper. A professional firm will deliver a professional response, even if it's a simple one-page letter with attached copies of the system documentation or sales material.

Very few if any vendor responses will look good and not be responsive. Vendors, as a general rule, will not waste their time on responding to a request when they know they cannot meet the needs. The problem is that if such a proposal is submitted, it could be disastrous for you to buy that product. Of course the evaluation itself should tell you if the system meets your needs. But what if you can't evaluate the response? What if the proposal seems to skirt the issues or tries to sell you a system other than the one you requested? Be careful! One indicator of such a proposal is the number of calls you must make to the vendor in order to understand the proposal. If it takes more than two or three calls then perhaps the proposal does not address your needs.

Most *canned or packaged programs* will often require some minor changes to fit very specific needs, such as Mr. Jones' special accounts receivable summaries, which he required to supply data to the general ledger. If, however, the vendor is proposing even minor changes to very general requirements, then you should proceed with caution. An accounts receivable system that requires modifications in order to add a service charge to an account or to print your customer statements is not a good buy. There are too many vendors with very good accounts receivable packages.

In short, don't worry about how to recognize an Edsel. Any businessperson running a successful business will recognize a nonresponsive proposal. The best approach is to study the responses and use common sense. You'll recognize a bad proposal when you read it!

SUMMARIZING THE FINALISTS

The final objective of the evaluation process is to identify those proposed systems that will meet your company's needs; it is not to choose the best single system. In most cases there will be two or more systems that clearly meet the requirements, but there may be only one or even none. Although Mr. Jones received four proposals for the inventory system, he found that none of the vendors proposed a system that offered the *Retail Inventory Method*, which was essential to his inventory system. As a result, he ruled out every inventory system proposed.

When all the applications have been evaluated and listings prepared of those proposed systems that meet the company's needs, then the candidates should be summarized by vendor on one list. Figure 10.3 is Bob Jones' list. This summary pointed out to Bob that Quick Systems' proposal, as a whole, was very strong. Note that Quick Systems had good systems in each of the application areas except inventory. Bob added his notes from the initial review to the right-hand column of the summary sheet. After studying the summary sheet he decided to drop Quality Systems and Every System Inc. because he had several proposals that met his requirements and both Quality Systems and Every System Inc. had borderline proposals.

In general, however, a vendor should not be dropped after having made the final candidates' list unless there are several good candidates and there is a clear reason to consider the system being dropped inferior to the other proposed systems.

There are several major reasons why purchasing all your software from the same vendor is a good practice. Usually maintenance costs and response time will improve if you have several packages from the same vendor. Also, the disputes over whose problem it is when two systems do not interface correctly is eliminated

FIGURE 10-3. Overall Proposal Evaluation Summary

Vendor	Retail Inventory (DROP)	Accounts Receivable	Accounts Payable	General Ledger	Total	Notes
Quick Systems	Not Acceptable 0 pts	Good candidate 90 pts	Good in all aspects 95 pts	Nice clean Interfacing 90 pts	275	Top candidate! good all around software
Mainframe		too cheap lots of changes required 40 pts	Acceptable 60 pts	Stand Alone No Interfacing 70 pts	170	Too cheap. appears better for small shop.
Improved Paper Products		Good people is big plus. Good software 90 pts	very workable system 95 pts	nice package but interfacing missing 85 pts	270	I like these people! Good packages
National Software	Does not have correct Inv. method. 0 pts	over all good. operates on 6 computers. 80 pts	nice working system 90 pts	Acceptable not very clear to operate 85 pts	255	pretty good all around.
Quality Systems	Good but no Retail Inventory option 30 pts	Good software poor salesman 75 pts	ok system not too smooth operating 85 pts	Simple system will require changes 70 pts	230	Acceptable poor sales person and some changes required
Every System Inc.	Nice for smaller firm. No Retail Method 15 pts	Good manuals Not willing to Assist. 75 pts	Special checks required otherwise good 85 pts	System ok. No conversion help. 75 pts	235	Good Documentation and nice systems but not help in installing

completely. These are factors you should consider before you complete the list that contains the final evaluation candidates; that is, those proposals that you feel meet your requirements and deserve further consideration.

All vendors who submitted proposals should be notified as to whether they made the final evaluation list. During this call, or shortly thereafter, arrangements should be made to have a demonstration prepared in preparation for the final decision. The demonstration, what to look for, and how to arrange it is the topic of the next chapter.

GLOSSARY

Canned Package Self-contained programs that perform a specific function such as payroll, accounts receivable, and accounts payable.

Final Evaluation List A list of vendors who have been selected to demonstrate their software. It contains the finalists in the search for the "right" software package.

Letter of Inquiry A letter sent from a vendor to a prospective customer asking for more information or clarification concerning the nature of a requested computer system.

Proposal The document prepared by a hardware or software vendor outlining how the vendor's computer system will satisfy the potential buyer's needs. A proposal is generally offered in response to the buyer's request and addresses the needs outlined in the buyer's requirements document. See Request For Proposal and Requirements Document.

Request for Proposal A document generally consisting of a vendor letter and requirements documents that is sent to vendors to request that they prepare a proposal to meet the customer's needs. See Vendor Letter and Requirements Document.

Retail Inventory Method An accounting process for inventory valuation and sales-cost calculation which works on an average-cost basis. This method starts with a base ratio of sales price to cost and uses that to estimate cost of goods sold given total sales at retail.

Vendor Evaluation Sheet A document prepared to allow comparison of the characteristics of various vendor proposals.

THE DEMONSTRATIONS: WHAT TO LOOK FOR

11

The electrical-supply store owner was dreading having to choose a small-business computer. He had worked hard to identify his choices, but his methods were erratic. He had decided that the best approach to finding a computer system would be to visit all the stores in town until one stood out as being better than all the rest. To date, he had seen seven computers and countless software packages. Was he ever confused! He had not kept many notes on what he had seen, so the demonstrations were all running together in his mind. To be sure, some of the packages had excellent capabilities, but what was the best combination? Tired of the whole process and under pressure from his bookkeeper to make a decision, this small-business owner contacted the computer vendor with the salesperson he liked most and made his purchase. Unfortunately, the software he ended up with was not capable of meeting his unique reporting needs and of growing with his business. The entire system was replaced two years later.

The small-business owner in the preceding example typifies some of the mistakes many people make when purchasing a small-business system. There are, however, some important lessons you can learn from his misfortune. The first place where this small-system owner failed was that he did not do his homework prior to the demonstrations. This has been covered in detail in previous chapters, and if the businessperson had followed such an approach, he would not have needed to see seven different computers. The second mistake he made was that he did not arrange the demonstrations to his maximum benefit. Instead, he wandered in "off the street" and was shown a demonstration befitting his preparation. Finally, this small businessman failed to walk away from the demonstrations with enough information for him to evaluate and compare the systems prior to making his final decision.

What is the best way to prepare for a vendor demonstration? You have already read about the steps in preparing a needs analysis and how to turn that into a requirements document. The demonstration is the place where all of the homework pays off. You should call the vendors selected during the vendor response process and arrange your demonstration. To accomplish this, the demonstration should be performed at a place where you can see live data demonstrated. If the software is installed at another company, that is the place to go see the system demonstration. If that is not an option, at least arrange to have a block of time set aside for you. There are few things as frustrating as trying to make a decision on a system while the demonstrator is helping more than one customer. Avoid large presentations where many companies are invited. You will be too inhibited to ask all the questions you need to ask.

When you schedule the visits to the various vendors, space them so that you see a demonstration every other day. The mental effort in seeing and comparing different systems and at the same time trying to fend off sales pitches makes it difficult to comfortably and effectively accomplish more than one every other day. It should take no more than half an hour to one and a half hours per application for the demonstration. More time than this means that you are seeing an inefficiently run presentation, which may mean that the salesperson does not know the system very well. You should arrange in advance to have the most important user of each system accompany you to the demonstrations. This is the point where their input concerning the usability is essential. If timing is difficult, at least arrange to have the major users visit your most likely candidate and get a feel for the user's likes and dislikes.

When you arrive at the demonstration, you should have several items at hand. First, you should bring the vendor proposal along with any questions you may have concerning maintenance, conversion assistance, and the like. This is the time to have those points cleared up. Also, you should take a copy of your requirements document to serve as a reference guide if any questions arise during the demonstration. You should review the points on the requirements document prior to the demonstration and also prepare a "hit list" of items to be covered in the demonstration. The hit list will keep your thoughts straight during the demonstration. Remember, however, that you want to see more than just your major requirement features demonstrated. All points on the requirements document are important at this stage, since this is the last opportunity you will have to see the system in action prior to making your final decision.

When the demonstration is presented, there are some points to keep in mind which will increase the effectiveness of the process. First, make sure that information used in the demonstration is taken from the point of input to the final reports. Do not be satisfied by seeing "how to enter data," followed by some sample reports. Only by following sample information from input screen to completed report with all intermediate steps included can you get a true feel for how the system operates. In fact, you may want to bring some actual documents which will be used as input to the system so you can see how easy it is to enter the information into the system. This may be more difficult if you are seeing a demonstration at a client site, but even in that case the demonstrator should be able to show test data flow through the software before showing you some actual reports created by the client company. The second thing to do during a demonstration is to keep notes. After your third demonstration you will be glad you have notes to refer to. Prepare one sheet of notes per application demonstrated. The following is a list of points to include on your demonstration sheet:

A. Hit list of points to be covered
   (prepared in advance)

B. Sections with places to make notes

- Does the salesperson know the system
- Are the screens easy to use
- Are the reports laid out well
- What hardware is supported
- What other systems does this interface to
- How good is the documentation
- Questions not covered in vendor's proposal (maintenance, conversion assistance, and so on)
- General impression of demonstration

The remarks you make will help you in your later evaluative process.
   The final thing to do when seeing a demonstration is to get questions answered that were raised when you received the vendor's proposal. For instance, if the proposal and its documentation did not cover certain features you requested, then you should ask about their availability when you receive the demonstration. This is your last chance to clear up questions before you have to make a choice. Similarly, it is just as important to question features noted on the proposal which you did not request and either do not want or do not understand. In short, make sure that the system meets the requirements you have laid out. Your guide in this entire process is the requirements document. No feature on that document is too small to question at this point. Although there is probably not a system that will meet all your requirements, you won't know which is the closest fit unless you ask all the questions.

ABC HARDWARE

Bob Jones began his demonstration process by calling Mainframe Computers. In the phone conversation, Bob asked if he could see the application systems in use at one of the vendor's client locations. Henry Higgins, Mainframe's small-business account rep, called Bob back and arranged a meeting at Anchor Auto Parts. When Bob arrived at Anchor, he was carrying the Mainframe proposal, his requirements document, some input documents his bookkeeper had given him, and three demonstration sheets. Bob had prepared one demonstration sheet for each of the application systems (receivables, payables, and general ledger). The hit list items on each sheet were the result of comparing the Mainframe proposal to his requirements document. There were also spaces on the sheet to write general comments.

When he arrived at Anchor, Bob was escorted to a side room where the Microframe II computer was kept. There he met Judy Conners, Anchor's bookkeeper, who ran the systems. Bob's first thought as he walked into the room was that the system was certainly making a lot of noise. He immediately noted this fact on one of the demonstration sheets. This would be an important consideration since Bob had originally planned to keep the system in the bookkeeping area at ABC, but now that appeared to be less feasible. The demonstration started slowly because Judy Connors was called to go help with a credit approval and Henry could not start up the first application, accounts receivable. Bob noted this fact under salesperson knowledge. He was already concerned about Mainframe's ability to provide support to its small-systems users, and the demonstration glitches just added to his concern.

Bob had brought some sample sales tickets to enter into the receivables system, but Connors had now returned and it was decided that first she would show Bob how she used the receivables package. Then Bob would be given a blank diskette to try his hand at running the system. Bob watched as Conners entered sales slips from a stack beside the machine. After several had been entered, Bob wrote on the receivables demonstration sheet "entry of sales slips easy to understand."

Next, Judy showed Bob how to set up a new customer on the receivables system. Again Bob was impressed by how easy the software was to use. Then the Anchor bookkeeper showed Bob how to print customer statements and reports. The process required a sorting process that took several minutes and then the printing began. Soon Bob noted a problem with the system. Every few minutes, Judy would have to stop the printer and line up the forms again to keep the printing inside the various boxes on the customer statements. Bob made a note of this problem. He would want a better printer.

When the printing was finished, Connors put in a new diskette for Bob to use, excused herself again, and Bob sat down to try his hand at entering his own sales tickets. Henry Higgins had been relatively quiet after his first failure to make the system respond, but now he began to tell Bob about the various features of the Mainframe accounts receivable package. Bob listened as he repeated the steps Connors had taken. Occasionally Higgins interrupted Bob to show him a better way to use the system. This indicated that Higgins really did know something about the software. When he was finished, Bob had added two more comments to his receivables demonstration sheet. Although he liked the menu-driven features of the system after he got used to how it operated, they were a nuisance and could not be bypassed. The second note was that the keyboard was uncomfortable and could not be positioned as easily as could those of other small-business computers he had seen.

Bob ended his demonstration of receivables by pulling out the requirements document and the Mainframe proposal. He had penciled some hit-list questions on the demonstration sheet concerning customer capacity, upgrade ability, interfacing, and summary balances maintained. Higgins answered these questions satisfactorily. Next, however, Bob asked about conversion support, and, as he expected, found out that ABC Hardware would be on its own to convert to the system. Fortunately there was some documentation covering the conversion steps.

Bob continued his demonstration by seeing the general ledger and payables packages. For each system he kept notes on a demonstration sheet. At the end of two hours, he left Anchor Auto Parts feeling satisfied that he had asked enough questions to make his decision and that he had sufficient documentation of what he had seen. A sample of one of the demonstration sheets Bob prepared follows in Table 11-1.

TABLE 11.1 Demonstration Sheet—Mainframe Accts Receivable

Hit List

1. What is the maximum # of customers? *1500*

2. Can we go from a Microframe II to another computer easily as our business grows? *yes, to Miniframe I*

TABLE 11.1. Demonstration Sheet (cont.)

3. At what levels does A/R interface with G/L?

See below

4. Are company overall totals maintained?

yes

Salesman's knowledge: *Higgins didn't know how to start up A/R; he improved as we got into it.*

Screen ease of use: *Great! Easy to use entering sales slips and new customers.*

Report layouts: *Good; statements could look better.*

Hardware supported: *Microframe II had 2 disk drives, a printer, and an extra terminal at anchors*

Interfacing: *Automatic to G/L (totals may be carried at various levels.)*

Documentation: *Manuals seemed complete, has 800 telephone No. for Questions!*

Conversion assistance: *Conversion Manuals only!*

General impressions: *Loud! High noise level in computer area. May require separate room.*

GLOSSARY

Live Data A term for information or data that is actually taken from your business, for example, payroll data from your personnel department.

MAKING THE FINAL DECISION

12

As was mentioned in Chapter 4 on "Surveying the Market," whether your company already has a computer or not can become an important factor in the number of options you have in choosing software. Chapter 10 indicated that hardware requirements (make, size, and cost) should become an important factor in determining your final group of software candidates. Of course if your hardware is predetermined then the entire task of finding and buying good software can become more difficult. This is basically true due to the limited number of software products available on any given type of hardware. Before making your final decision you should become very familiar with the hardware you are considering. If you already have equipment, you should know most of the factors to be considered. If you are not committed to hardware, then now is the time to familiarize yourself with it. You have already made three visits to the computer stores and you have seen each system operate. If at this time, however, you are still uncomfortable with one or more of the computers being considered, resolve that situation now. This is a good time to contact some of the references that vendors gave you and to talk with friends and associates about the dependability of the hardware being proposed.

    If you discover reasons to question the reliability of a particular manufacturer, then eliminate it immediately. With recent improvements in hardware, most mini- and microcomputers are reliable. You may, however, find a situation where local maintenance or support is not available. If you find local users who are dissatisfied or disappointed in the hardware's performance, then you have a good reason to eliminate those software packages that are required to operate on that particular equipment. Good software that runs on poor hardware is not an option.

    From this point on it is assumed that the hardware question has been answered. Either you are already committed to particular equipment or you are reasonably satisfied with the various hardware options remaining on your list of software finalists. The only remaining question is which package or set of packages (if more than one application is being considered) is best. How you determine the final choice will depend upon whether you are looking for the best single application or whether your search included several applications simultaneously. As we will soon see, Bob Jones of ABC Hardware learned this lesson the hard way by first choosing the best accounts receivable package, then having to choose the best combination of accounts receivable, accounts payable, payroll, and general ledger packages.

CHOOSING THE BEST SINGLE APPLICATION

In many cases where only one application is being considered the final decision on which software package to buy becomes an easy process. It is not uncommon, and you should not be concerned, if, in the final analysis, there is only one proposal that is truly outstanding or even just acceptable. This is especially true if your requirements are unique or are in a field in which the microcomputer has barely penetrated the market. In many instances there may be no software available at all, and other approaches, such as having to develop a system or make major modifications to a "close fit" system, are the only solutions. Both of these alternatives are costly, but could result in a very marketable product. In either case very serious consideration and evaluation should be made before departing from a "canned" package.

If you complete the final demonstrations stage and still have no clear-cut choice, then making the final decision can become difficult. The best approach at this stage is to do what Bob Jones did in his first pass at making a final decision for ABC Hardware. Bob developed a *decision matrix* and tried to rate the finalists based upon value judgments on each system's strengths and weaknesses. This is a good approach for making a single-application decision.

In considering the accounts receivable system, Bob had difficulty deciding between the Quick Systems, Improved Paper Products, and National Software packages. To help in his decision he wrote down the following items, which he felt were important decision factors:

- Extra Hardware Costs
- Software Costs
- Total Costs
- Annual Maintenance Costs
- Location of Hardware Maintenance
- Location of Software Maintenance

Making the Final Decision • **125**

- Compatible with Other Chosen Software
- Special Environmental Requirements
- Program Modification Requirements

Bob's previous choices for software already dictated what hardware he would buy. As a result, the only hardware cost he had to consider was the additional equipment that would be needed if he purchased each package. Across the top of his decision matrix he listed the names of the three vendors being considered, with space after each name. In the space he rated each package. Figure 12.1 shows the decision matrix.

Next he made comments on each factor for each vendor and summarized his finding in the matrix. When the entire matrix was filled, he subjectively rated the three companies as strong (+), acceptable (0), and weak (−). When he could not decide if one was better than another he rated both the same. On extra hardware cost he rated all three as strong, since he considered the hardware cost variances to be less significant. He next evaluated the entire matrix, eventually eliminating the National Software package because their rating was considerably below the quality of the other two. He was particularly concerned that their software maintenance location was several hundred miles from his business location. Given that all three software packages were acceptable, he did not like the idea of out-of-state maintenance when closer service was available.

In the final analysis between the Improved Paper Products' and Quick Systems' accounts receivable packages, Bob chose the Improved Paper Products offer. He knew he would be happy with either package, but the personnel at Improved Paper Products seemed more aggressively interested in his account and he felt a closer working relationship could be developed with them. He particularly liked the programmer whom he was told would be responsible for making programming modifications for him. Bob's only hesitation with Improved Paper Products was that they were a paper manufacturer and not a software house. Because of this concern he contacted five of the eight references Improved Paper Products had given him. All five were users of the Improved Paper Products' accounts receivable system and he received outstanding reviews of both the software and the company's data processing staff.

Since ABC Hardware would be Improved Paper Products' largest software customer, Bob felt good about his choice. It was not until he began evaluating the payroll, accounts payable, and general ledger proposals that he discovered his problem.

FIGURE 12-1. Single Application Decision Matrix

	QUICK SYSTEMS	+/o/-	IMPROVED PAPER PRODUCTS	+/o/-	NATIONAL SOFTWARE	+/o/-
EXTRA HARDWARE COST	None	+	None	+	None	+
SOFTWARE COSTS	24,200	o	25,070	o	20,050	+
TOTAL COSTS	24,200	o	25,070	o	20,050	o
ANNUAL MAINT. COSTS	2,500	+	2,400	+	3,600	-
LOCATION OF HARDWARE MAINT.	50 Miles Away	+	In Town	+	Out-of-state	-
LOCATION OF SOFTWARE MAINT.	50 Miles Away	+	In Town	+	Kansas City-80 Miles	-
COMPATABILITY WITH OTHER SOFTWARE	Excellent! With All Applications.	+	Only General Ledger is a Problem.	+	All Independent of General Ledger and Each Other.	o
SPECIAL ENVORONMENTAL REQUIREMENTS	None	+	None	+	None	+
PROGRAM MODIFICATION REQUIREMENTS	None	+	Very Minor - For General Ledger Only	+	Same to Interface General Ledger	+
		+7		+7		+1

MAKING A MULTIPLE-APPLICATION DECISION

In a single-application decision the major objective is to find the best single software package that meets, as a minimum, every requirement set out in the requirements document. Usually, even if there are several packages that meet the requirements, one proposal will stand out. On occasion there may be more, but even then there is no consideration given to choosing the second or third best. The objective is to pick the single best package. With multiple-application decisions the objective remains the same but the complexity of the decision increases. Other factors become important and the final decision becomes not which single software package is best for each given application but rather which series of packages combine to make the best overall system. In this situation it is not always the best package for any one given application that is chosen. It may, in fact, be the second or even third best, depending upon the other factors that come into play with multiple-application decisions.

As mentioned in Chapter 10, "Evaluating Vendor Responses," hardware can play an important role, particularly in the multi-application evaluation. The best system for one application may run on a different computer than the best system for another application. This can cause you to have to pick a second or third choice.

A very important factor in a multi-application evaluation is the coupling factor between the applications. Coupling is a word often used by computer technicians to refer to the dependency of certain programs or subprograms to one another. If there is a strong inner relationship between the various applications, say between accounts payable and general ledger, then the two can be referred to as "tightly coupled," that is, one or both packages depend on each other. An example of tightly coupled applications might be an accounts payable package that takes all the data that has been entered into the system and automatically reformats and transmits the information in some form to the general ledger package.

If the two applications are independent of each other, then they are referred to as "loosely coupled." Any application that is totally independent of the other can, for all practical purposes, be chosen as a single-applications decision. Of course, the fact that all the applications must execute on the same type of equipment makes them, at least, loosely coupled. If, however, the hardware choice has already been made, they can still be considered as independent single-application decisions, assuming that hardware was their commonality.

If you have a requirement that two or more applications interface, then you will have coupling. It is best to reduce coupling to a minimum without eliminating the interfacing all together. Sending summary-level transactions, for example, from the payroll system to the general ledger is better than sending detailed transactions of every employee on the payroll. Better, that is, unless your requirements absolutely demand that level of detail, in which case, of course, tightly coupled applications will be a must. One advantage of keeping the interrelationship between applications at a minimum is that the cost of having a programmer develop the interface can be greatly reduced. If tightly coupled applications are required you may be forced to accept both systems from the same vendor, whether or not they are each singularly the best package.

After choosing Improved Paper Products' accounts receivable package, Bob felt comfortable enough with his approach and the vendors that he decided to evaluate the payroll, accounts payable, and general ledger proposals together. His primary reason for taking the *multiple-application decision* approach was the interfacing requirements. He wanted all the applications to automatically feed the general ledger.

His first step was to develop a single-application decision matrix similar to the one he used on accounts receivable (Figure 12.1). Next he prepared a summary matrix that he could use to summarize the detail matrices, and he added considerations such as overall costs, interfacing, demonstration impressions, and the like. Since he had already prepared an accounts receivable single-decision matrix, he added accounts receivable to the multiple-decision matrix. The resulting matrix is shown in Figure 12.2. After Bob completed his multiple-application evaluation of all four applications, he came to appreciate the differences between evaluating software for one application versus several applications at one time.

Reviewing the summary matrix, Bob again eliminated National Software because of their long-distance maintenance requirements. Although he wanted Improved Paper Products to win the entire bid process, after studying the matrix he felt the overall best proposal was unquestionably Quick Systems. But this presented a problem because of the coupling requirement he had between the accounts receivable and the general ledger. Improved Paper Products' accounts receivable package would not interface with Quick Systems'

FIGURE 12-2. Multiple Application Decision Matrix

	QUICK SYSTEMS	IMPROVED PAPER PRODUCTS	RATIONAL SOFTWARE
HARDWARE COSTS	+	+	+
PAYROLL	+	+	o
ACCTS/RECV.	o	+	-
ACCTS/PAYABLE	+	o	o
GENERAL LEDGER	+	o	o
TOTAL COSTS	+	o	o
INTERFACING TO G/L	+	o	-
DOCUMENTATION	+	+	+
DEMO IMPRESSION	+	+	o

general ledger. To be fair Bob called Improved Paper Products and received a cost estimate of $6,500 for them to modify their accounts receivable package so it could transfer summary data to the Quick Systems' general ledger. The added cost changed Bob's mind on the accounts receivable decision, and ABC Hardware chose to accept Quick Systems' entire proposal for all systems. Bob was disappointed but he felt he had made the right decision.

Before he bought, Bob performed two very key financial evaluations. He met with his accountant and tried to identify any hidden costs involved with his decision to automate. Then he and his accountant determined the best ways to "book" his investment. These two important topics are covered in Chapters 13 and 14.

Less than a week after making his final decision, Bob signed a check consigned to Quick Systems, and ABC Hardware began planning to implement its new small-business software.

(The implementation process is the topic of the authors' next book, entitled: *The Microcomputer Implementation Cookbook*. The book follows Bob Jones through the planning, preparation, and installation stages of ABC Hardware's implementation project.)

GLOSSARY

Coupling A term used in relating the dependency of two or more entities, such as programs or packages. "Tightly coupled" refers to packages in which at least one software package must pass important data to the other in order for the second to function properly. "Loosely coupled" refers to two packages that can, but not necessarily must, pass data. No coupling occurs when the packages do not transfer data between each other.

Decision Matrix A matrix listing vendors and requirements that are being evaluated. The purpose of the matrix is to give an overview of the proposals and how they meet the requirements. The objective is to eliminate nonresponsive proposals.

Detailed Transactions Transactions that carry detail information. For example, a detailed payroll transaction may carry the withholding taxes, gross pay, and medical deductions for a single employee. See *Summary Level Transactions*.

Loosely Coupled See *Coupling*.

Multiple-Application Decision A step-by-step approach or methodology for determining the best proposed software packages for a multiple-application decision. For example, how to determine the best proposal for a combination payroll, accounts receivable, and general ledger system. See *Single-Application Decision*.

Single-Application Decision A step-by-step approach or methodology for determining the best proposed software package for a single application, such as payroll. See *Multiple-Application Decision*.

Software House A computer company that specializes in developing computer software packages. A programming company that develops application software.

Summary-Level Transactions Transactions that carry summary data found in more detail transactions. For example, a summary-level payroll transaction may carry the total withholding taxes and total gross pay for all employees in a certain department. See *Detailed Transactions*.

Tightly Coupled See *Coupling*.

RECOGNIZING HIDDEN COSTS

13

The local wholesaler was ecstatic two months ago. His operations were being more accurately monitored and he was receiving reports that kept him on top of his business. But now he was facing two problems. First, the company that had manufactured the small-business computer he had purchased announced a more advanced product for just about the same price soon after his was installed. He had no complaints about his computer's performance that would make him want to trade up, but this turn of events upset his plans to keep the system for at least five years. He knew when he read that his computer was being discontinued that service would be diffficult to obtain in the near future.

Even more pressing were his space problems. Like most small businesses, this firm had outgrown its buildings, but now the problem was exacerbated by having to dedicate an entire room to the new computer. Not only that, but a new air conditioner had to be installed to compensate for the heat that the unusually large system generated. This combination of cramping his office employees and the costs and discomfort of keeping one room at a cooler temperature than the rest of the office made the owner think that maybe it was time to add more space or move. What had happened to his plan of staying in his current building for at least three more years? Both of these problems are examples of hidden costs of owning a small-business computer. Unfortunately, obsolescence and space considerations are not the only hidden expenses this small-business owner will encounter during the years he owns his computer.

What are the other hidden costs of owning a small-business system? This chapter is a postscript that discusses some of the items that are usually not considered prior to purchasing a small-business computer, but which undoubtedly add significantly to the monthly costs of ownership. The intent is not to stop you from buying, because just as surely as there are costs of ownership, there are also costs associated with not owning a small-business computer when you need one. Rather, the purpose is to inform. Many small businesses operate on tight cash budgets without the additional expenses associated with small-business computers. By being forewarned of the forthcoming expenses, you can at least budget more effectively. For discussion purposes, we will break these expenses down into the areas of personnel, building, maintenance, and special equipment costs. Each area will be explored in more detail in the following pages.

PERSONNEL

There are several hidden costs in the area of personnel. First, let's consider what the "people" concerns are with a small-business computer. Many of the requirements for personnel time depend on the type of system purchased. For instance, if your computer is a small unit with only one terminal and you plan to run a limited number of application programs, then you can probably get by with training your existing personnel to use the new computer. Note, however, that there are some costs associated with this training. These costs take two forms. First, there is the time spent reading manuals or perhaps even attending a formal training program. Too many times small-business computer owners assume that the required skills of running their new machine can be picked up from an hour or so of looking over a manual. The procedure will be too dissimilar to your employees' normal functions for this assumption to be valid. You should think of training costs as insurance against problems of the future. There are also costs involved with the other employees who are forced to cover for the person learning about the new machine. The second cost is associated with time lost when the computer or software malfunctions, as it inevitably will, and your employees are left without needed information. These are only a few of the problems of working with such sophisticated equipment.

If your system is a larger, *multi-terminal* unit, then you should probably consider hiring a full-time person to operate the computer. This serves two functions. First it keeps your other personnel from becoming frustrated when the *computer is down*. Having a full-time computer operator who is trained in maintaining your machine can make minor technical difficulties more manageable. After all, you do not want your entire staff waiting on a repairman who may be two to four hours away from your office. A second point in favor of having a full-time operator is that if you have a large system configuration then you have a fair amount of money invested, which means that you want a higher level of performance. Your operator can learn how to program and thus learn to make modifications to your software so it can be tailored to your individual business needs. Having such a person may be necessary, but just as with training costs, the effect on the bottom line should not be ignored.

BUILDING

Building costs take several forms. First, as was mentioned in the opening example, you must not forget to consider that floor space must be dedicated to your machine. The amount required again depends on the specifications of the computer you have selected. As you would expect, the larger the computer and the more devices attached to it, the more floor space it requires. Do not be misled by claims for "desk-top" and "workstation" units, although these smaller units certainly do meet the advertised space savings. Most businesspeople are hard-pressed to find an employee who will want to sacrifice desk space for a computer. Inevitably the machine will have to be allocated its own table and locale. That takes space!

There are other building costs associated with being a small-business computer owner. For systems on the high end of the small-business computer scale there will be requirements for air conditioning to keep the machine within its *operating constraints*. (Fortunately, this is becoming less common as computer engineering progresses.) If the air conditioning requirements, along with the number of cables it takes to hook up a computer to multiple users and devices, become a large enough problem you will probably be better advised to consider building a special computer room with its own air conditioning unit, power supply, and raised floor. Again, this is only necessary for someone who wants a lot from a small-business computer and consequently must purchase a machine with a lot of "horsepower."

MAINTENANCE AND OBSOLESCENCE COSTS

One of the major continuing costs of owning a small-business computer is the expense of maintaining the machinery. It is a fact of computer ownership that these machines can break down, and, in fact, do so with frustrating regularity. Horror stories abound, and you have certainly heard, read, or experienced at least one if you have followed the prescribed procedures for becoming familiar with computers as outlined in the first part of this book. Realizing this inevitability, it is the prudent small-computer owner who plans for these problems so as to minimize their impact.

First, you should understand why computers break down. After all, you are saying, are these computers not built with the supposedly infallible microelectronic technology of today? The answer to this question is mostly yes. Unfortunately, two devices, printers and disk drives, still contain a large proportion of mechanical parts connected to the sophisticated microelectronics. A printer's mechanism for printing receives a large amount of wear and tear in the process of preparing your daily reports. Similarly, a disk drive, as it sits and turns, waiting for a request for data storage or retrieval, uses up a large portion of its limited life cycle.

In both cases it is inevitable that the device will some day require maintenance. Unfortunately that day of reckoning is hastened in many small businesses by two factors. First, many small-business owners shorten the effective lives of their computers through misuse and abuse. Read the enclosed instructions and follow them closely! Also, there is sometimes a tendency to purchase *peripheral* equipment from the low end of the market. With computer equipment, as with most things, you get what you pay for. That cheaper printer is many times less expensive for a reason—it was not engineered or built to take the punishment that its larger and more expensive cousins are capable of withstanding.

Along with maintenance costs go the implicit costs of obsolescence. It is a two-edged sword that has cleared the path for lower-priced microcomputers in business. Although it is fortunate that these machines have come along in time to ease many of the information-processing burdens of the small-business owner, they have also brought with them the hidden costs of becoming nonfunctional rather rapidly. This obsolescence can occur in two ways. First, a short product life can be brought on by leaps in computer technology. With the funding, research, and manufacturing efforts that have been turned toward producing smaller, more powerful, and yet cheaper computers, it is obvious that the product life cycle of a microcomputer is going to be much shorter than that of other office machinery of the past.

Another factor contributing to the problem of obsolescence is the changing makeup of the computer manufacturers themselves. It can be said with some assurance that a shakeout is going to occur among microcomputer manufacturers. The number of small-business systems being manufactured is staggering. Five years from now there will not be such a confusing array of products, but there will be confusion among the small businesses which own systems that are no longer manufactured. The winning manufacturers will probably not comprise the most technologically advanced entries either. Rather, they will be soundly managed and financially secure companies that could afford to change with the industry.

You may be wondering what the significance of this obsolescence is as long as the costs are low enough that you can afford to scrap the machine when a better product comes along. The problem with this approach is that in the process of being a small-business computer owner you also become a software and *data file* owner. In short, you have a rather significant investment in software products and in data maintained in the format to allow those programs to run. If at the end you find that your computer manufacturer has folded and now makes widgets, you must scrap everything and convert to a new machine. This conversion process can be both difficult and expensive. Even if the company is still around (but your machine is no longer manufactured), you will have problems. Software companies write programs for the largest markets. Once your machine is discontinued, you find a steadily shrinking source of software products along with the expected problems of spare parts and maintenance difficulties.

The lesson from all this is simple to understand but hard to put into practice. Choose a computer manufacturer whom you expect to be around five years from now and avoid the problem of the businessman discussed at the beginning of this chapter by not buying a computer that will likely be replaced soon. This second part is the most tricky. If you buy a computer too early in its life cycle, there is little software and there may even be a few engineering problems left to be worked out. However, if you wait too long in the life cycle, you have an obsolescence problem. You want a machine after it has matured, but while it still has some years left to go. Good luck!

PERIPHERAL EQUIPMENT

The final area of hidden costs found with small-business computers concerns the peripheral equipment that is used with them. It is unfortunate that most small-business computer purchasers spend a large percentage of their decision-making time pondering the advantages and disadvantages of the various CPUs. This is not good because it is the peripheral equipment that has the largest amount of maintenance and other continuing costs associated with it. These pieces of machinery should receive a larger share of the purchase consideration.

The printer has already been discussed in relation to its maintenance costs. It also has a high cost of care and feeding. Printers consume large amounts of paper and ribbons as they perform their daily functions. They also require products for containing and filing the reports and listings produced. These products are not cheap. Costs are coming down, but computer supplies are still very high. Disk drive units are no better. Not only do they require an expensive collection of magnetic disks, but they also require storage facilities with the proper combination of temperature, humidity, and absence of magnetic fields from other equipment. Disks also have a habit of multiplying, as you find that you cannot purge last year's files while waiting for an audit or to save comparison information. The rule of thumb is that the number of disks required is directly proportional to, and in fact always seems to exceed, the number available.

CONCLUSION

The fact that microcomputers are like any other piece of machinery and require some continuing care and expense probably is not a surprise to you. Because these machines are so new, the areas in which the costs arise will probably be new, and thus may have caught you unaware. There is no way to avoid these expenses. As was mentioned earlier, if you need a microcomputer, the advantages of having this powerful tool far outweigh the disadvantages. It is important, though, to understand these costs and to budget appropriately.

GLOSSARY

Computer Is Down A phrase commonly used to mean that the computer system is not operating. The fault may lie with either the hardware or software.

Data File A collection of records or data that contains information in a format that a computer program can use.

Multi-Terminal The ability to have more than one terminal operating on one computer at the same time. Multi-terminal capabilities require both special hardware characteristics and software flexibility.

Operating Constraints Those characteristics of a computer's hardware that place requirements on its environment. Examples include operating temperature and humidity.

Peripheral A device that is external to the main frame of the computer. Generally, peripherals are used as input or output devices, such as printers, CRTs, and disk drives.

BOOKING YOUR INVESTMENT

14

You have just decided on a small-business computer and cannot wait to have it delivered. You've seen tremendous opportunities and imagine that once the machine is installed there will be other benefits available from having such computing power at your disposal. You also have just read about the hidden costs that are a part of owning a small-business computer. Having seen the positive and the negative points displayed side by side, it would be natural for you to wonder what costs are encountered when purchasing a small-business computer and how these costs are treated.

The purchase costs for a small-business computer may be broken down into hardware costs, software costs, and cost of a maintenance contract. The components of each depend on the particulars of your purchase, however, some general rules can be stated for the accounting and tax consequences. Also, there are some peculiarities based on whether you decide to purchase or lease your system components. The intent of this chapter is not to provide exact tax advice; you should see your accountant or tax consultant if you have questions. Rather, the purpose of this chapter is to provide some insight into the financing of and accounting for a computer purchase.

HARDWARE AND SOFTWARE

The hardware components of a small-business computer system can be discussed with one basic question in mind: do you want to lease or buy? If you already own business machinery, then this question is not new to you. Many businesspeople have not had extensive dealings with the choices involved, or have made the necessary decisions without embarking on a detailed analysis beforehand. It is to this group that the following discussion is addressed.

Let's consider the purchase option. When you purchase the hardware components of a small-business computer, there are two effects on your financial position. First, there is an immediate use of funds to purchase the machine. The second effect is that you receive part of these funds back in later years. This occurs through two tax devices: the investment tax credit and depreciation. The *investment tax credit* is taken in the year of purchase and its amount depends on the purchase price and the expected life of the machine. Depreciation is spread over the life of the system and allows you to systematically recover the cost of the machine against future revenues. There can also be some considerations for additional first-year depreciation, salvage value, and the possible recovery of the credit, but we are going to keep this discussion at its simplest level.

Leasing is very prevalent in the computer industry today. The lessor may be either the manufacturer itself, a third-party company that specializes in equipment leasing, or a financial institution. If the lease contains terms providing for transfer of the equipment at the end of the lease term, then it is what is known as a capital lease, and is in reality just another form of purchase financing. The lease payments in this case are structured to provide a rate of return or interest rate to the lessor. The lessor has the option of taking the investment tax credit or passing it on to you. The company will probably take the credit, however, as a component of the return on its investment. You have the right to depreciate the machinery, since you are purchasing it through your lease payments.

The second type of lease is known as an operating lease. Here the lessor retains the equipment at the end of the lease. The lessor company may also provide maintenance over the term of the lease if it is the manufacturer of the equipment. Although there are some sophisticated accounting rules that determine whether a lease is of the capital or operating variety, in most cases it is whether or not the title is transferred that makes the difference. Thus, an operating lease is basically a rental agreement. As such, the lessor will take both the investment tax credit and depreciation, and your only financial effects are the monthly lease payments. If you are looking for a small-business computer to be used in a nonprofit organization, then an operating lease may be preferable, since you cannot take advantage of the tax benefits such as investment tax credits and depreciation anyway.

When you are making your final decisions on software and hardware, you should begin to consider these financing options. One of the primary determinants of what options are available to you is the price of the equipment. Large-scale micro-systems have a higher price tag and the mechanisms for purchasing them have evolved in many directions. For instance, such a system may be available with a manufacturer's operating (rental) lease or you may purchase the machine and arrange your own financing or leasing arrangements with your bank or financial institution. With this size of system you can also find companies that specialize in third-party leasing. This involves an *operating lease* with the company for a set length of time. In cases in which you are leasing from the manufacturer or a third party, maintenance may be included in the lease payments, although this is not always available.

Lower-priced systems normally do not have all of these options. The reason is that there is not enough profit in leasing these systems for the manufacturers or third-party leasing companies. Some lease arrangements can be found for a few of the more popular low-end systems, but these are typically of the *capital lease* variety. This means that the lessor is just providing financing for your purchase. Since the rate of interest on such lease agreements is normally higher than prevailing bank rates, and since the lessor will probably also be taking the tax credit on the machines, you are usually better off to use your existing credit arrangements to make the purchase.

MAINTENANCE AGREEMENTS

One final point about hardware concerns maintenance agreements. Maintenance agreements are the arrangements between you and either the manufacturer or another servicing organization to provide continued service for your small-business system. The intent is to cover some of the types of maintenance arrangements that can be found on the market today.

With maintenance, as with other hardware considerations, it is the size of your system that to a large degree determines what is available. For instance, some large microcomputer companies offer maintenance contracts with guaranteed service response time and scheduled preventive maintenance. You can even find guaranteed uptime agreements in some maintenance contracts. These options do not come without a price. At the other end of the scale is the small micro, which must normally be carried back to the store where it was purchased for repairs. You can find maintenance contracts on these smaller machines, but when viewed in proportion to total purchase cost the price tag can be high.

Pricing of maintenance contracts depends on system sizes again. The large micro carries a high enough price tag that the manufacturer can provide service at a profit using a *percentage of purchase price* per month method. With the low-end micros, you normally find that companies offer fixed monthly price maintenance contracts. The percentage used for these less expensive microcomputers would have to be very large to cover the costs of maintaining the hardware.

ABC HARDWARE

When Bob Jones reached the point where he had made his final decision on software and hardware, he was forced to stop and consider the financing of his new system. Bob decided on a system that consisted of the following:

Computer, 2 terminals, 2 disk drives	$13,750
Software packages	$3,250
Maintenance contract with manufacturer; with a guaranteed 2-day response	$200/mo.

An alternative to an outright purchase of the machine is a lease from a third-party source, Lease-Comp. The Lease-Comp arrangement called for monthly payments of $1,100 on a one-year renewable lease. The lease covers hardware, software, and maintenance and Lease-Comp retains the computer at the end of the lease period.

Another important consideration was the fact that if Bob had purchased the computer, he could take an investment tax credit, something Lease-Comp did not offer. Also, Bob estimated that the useful life of this system would be five years and that it probably would have little if any value at the end of that time. His reason for making that decision was based on the fact that computer technology is changing rapidly and his machine will certainly be outmoded in five years.

EVALUATING THE OPTIONS

Evaluation of leasing versus purchasing options involves the use of a technique known as "discounted cash flow" analysis. The basic premise of this method is that a dollar received today is worth more than one received a year from now. You can also think of discounting as applying a time value to money. Basically, what happens using this technique is that the valuations of payments made in future years are reduced or "discounted." The discounting calculations are not very difficult. However, determining the numbers to use in the process requires a knowledge of both tax and finance.

Bob Jones, having neither of these backgrounds, decided to take his information to his accountant. The accountant showed Bob what his options were for the investment tax credit and for depreciating the investment. Bob was amazed to find how complicated the process was. Next, the accountant mapped the cash flows against time and compared them to those required for a lease arrangement. The accountant showed Bob that to accurately compare the two investments, he must consider the financing costs associated with purchasing the machine and include these costs in the cash flow analysis. Finally, the accountant explained to Bob that the analysis should be performed on an after-tax basis to net the effect of the investment tax credit and depreciation against the cash outflows.

At the end of the session with the accountant, Bob was glad that he had not tried to compare the two options himself. For one thing, the accountant had been able to give Bob accurate and current tax information which allowed him to save a considerable amount in lower tax payments. Also, the accountant had employed the discounted cash flow analysis and had shown Bob that in his case, it would be preferable for Bob to purchase the machine rather than to lease it. This did not cause Bob any problem since he had an adequate line of credit to finance both the computer and several other capital purchases that he was planning. Bob called the salesman and made arrangements for delivery!

GLOSSARY

Capital Lease A lease arrangement in which the lessor is in effect providing financing for the purchase of equipment by the person leasing the equipment. There are several ways in which a lease can be categorized as a capital lease, but the most common one is that ownership of the equipment passes to the lessee at the end of the lease term.

Discounted Cash-Flow Analysis A method for analyzing the effects of future cash inflows and outflows against the current investment cost. This method is based on the premise that a dollar received a year from now will be worth some amount less than a dollar received today.

Investment Tax Credit The income tax credit that is allowed on the purchase of equipment used for business purposes.

Operating Lease A lease agreement in which the lessor is in effect renting the equipment to the lessee for the term of the lease. Ownership of the equipment does not pass to the lessee at the end of the lease term.

Percentage of Purchase Price When used in reference to maintenance contracts, this term refers to a monthly maintenance amount, which is calculated as a percentage of the total purchase price of the equipment covered by the maintenance contract.

GLOSSARY

Abort When the computer reaches a point at which it can no longer continue processing, due either to unexpected or faulty data, or instructions to the computer that cannot be executed.

Account Balance Report A report of all balances maintained on an application system, such as accounts receivable, as of the report date.

Aged Accounts Report A report showing accounts receivable balances by customer with a breakdown by age of the amounts due.

BASIC A popular computer language that is often the main language on a microcomputer.

Byte A unit of measure equal to enough information to describe one letter, number, or character. The technical definition of byte can vary based upon the type of hardware.

Candidate for Automation A manual business accounting function such as payroll or inventory that is selected as a possible choice for automation by a computer-based system.

Canned or Packaged Programs Computer programs that are written for sale in a mass market to take advantage of economies in spreading the development costs over a wider base.

Capital Lease A lease arrangement in which the lessor is in effect providing financing for the purchase of equipment by the person leasing the equipment. There are several ways in which a lease can be categorized as a capital lease, but the most common one is that ownership of the equipment passes to the lessee at the end of the lease term.

Compile To translate a high-level language, such as COBOL or Pascal, into machine readable code that the computer can understand.

Computer Is Down A phrase commonly used to mean that the computer system is not operating. The fault may lie with either the hardware or software. See *Abort*.

Computer Languages Languages that people use to tell the computer what to do. Languages can be high-level (English-like) or low-level (closer to the computer's machine language). See *Low-Level Language* and *High-Level Language*.

Controller A controller is a hardware device that is used to control the communications between the computer and one or more peripheral devices. Information sent to a peripheral is intercepted by the controller and translated and timed so that the peripheral can be operated more efficiently.

Coupling A term used in relating the dependency of two or more entities, such as programs or packages. "Tightly coupled" refers to packages in which at least one software package must pass important data to the other in order for the second to function properly. "Loosely coupled" refers to two packages that can, but not necessarily must, pass data. No coupling occurs when the packages do not transfer data between each other.

CP/M A computer operating system that is widely used and accepted among microcomputer manufacturers. The advantage of a CP/M-based system is that there is a large variety of software available that executes under the CP/M operating system.

CPS An abbreviation for characters per second. CPS is a measurement for the speed in which a printer operates. For example, 30 CPS is considered slow. See *LPM*.

CPU An abbreviation for central processing unit. The CPU is the "brain" of the computer in that it is the hardware that performs the arithmetic and logical functions.

CRT Abbreviation for cathode ray tube, a peripheral device resembling a television which is used to display input and output information.

Daisy Wheel A circular printing device that is used on many printers to give the printer letter-quality capabilities. A daisy wheel printer is usually more durable and expensive than a dot matrix printer.

Data File A collection of records or data that contains information in a format that a computer program can use.

Decision Matrix A matrix listing vendors and requirements that are being evaluated. The purpose of the matrix is to give an overview of the proposals and how they meet the requirements. The objective is to eliminate nonresponsive proposals.

Detailed Activity Report A report showing the transactions that have been posted to the master files of an application, such as accounts receivable, during the current period.

Detailed Transactions Transactions that carry detailed information. For example, a detailed payroll transaction may carry the withholding taxes, gross pay, and medical deductions for a single employee. See *Summary Level Transactions*.

Discounted Cash-Flow Analysis A method for analyzing the effects of future cash inflows and outflows against the current investment cost. This method is based on the premise that a dollar received a year from now will be worth some amount less than a dollar received today.

Disk Drive A peripheral device that spins a record-type disk and stores and retrieves information on the disk's platter. The platter can be hard or flexible. See *Hard Disk* and *Floppy Disk*.

Documentation The collection of documents that provide information to the users of a computer system. The varieties of documentation typically found include maintenance, operating, and user.

Dot Matrix Printer A printer that uses small dots to form characters. Generally less expensive and less durable than a standard (daisy wheel) printer.

End User The individual who receives the final product (printed reports, displayed results, and the like) from the system.

Enhanced Graphics A printer or printing device that can print detail graphs, often in color.

Error-Code Table A table or glossary of all the errors that a program or system may encounter. Usually a short mnemonic code, such as PE02 (Programmer Error number 2) is given, followed by a detailed description of the error condition. The mnemonic codes are listed in alphabetical order for easy access.

Evaluation Form The document used in the evaluation of prospective hardware and software suppliers.

Final Evaluation List A list of vendors who have been selected to demonstrate their software. It contains the finalists in the search for the "right" software package.

Floppy Disk A thin, mylar, record-shaped disk housed in a protective cardboard jacket and used to store information and programs. Floppy disks have far less storage capacity than hard disks.

Generic Package A set of programs to perform a generalized accounting function, such as accounts payable, which does not have any industry-specific features. In other words, it will work generally well for most businesses, but may not meet all the needs of any one business.

Hands On A term that refers to a person's having access for operating the hardware equipment.

Hard Disk A standard, nonflexible, and often self-contained disk that can store from three million up to one billion characters of information.

Hardware The equipment and electrical components of a computer.

Hardware Independent A term used to refer to software that can be run on any machine without the software having to be modified. True hardware independence is very rare because of the lack of uniformity among hardware manufacturers.

Hardware Vendor The company that manufactures or assembles computer equipment.

High-Level Language Computer languages that are more English-like than are low-level languages. See *Computer Languages* and *Low-Level Language*.

High Resolution A terminal device (CRT or printer) that can print enhanced graphics because it has the ability to print more dots in each character's dot matrix than can a low-resolution dot matrix device. See *Dot Matrix Printer*.

Home and Personal Computers The smallest line of computers, these machines are generally defined as being priced under $5,000 and allow only one user at a time.

Input Collectively refers to the information that must be input into a computer system in order for the system to operate and maintain the necessary management information.

Interfacing When one software package prepares information in a format that can be used by another package without having to reenter the data through the keyboard.

Investment Tax Credit The income-tax credit that is allowed on the purchase of equipment used for business purposes.

K An abbreviation for *kilobyte*.

Keyboard That part of a peripheral device that is styled like a typewriter and is used to key information into the computer.

Kilobyte A unit of measure for information, which equals 1024 bytes, and is primarily used to describe internal or external storage capacities. See *Byte*.

Letter of Inquiry A letter sent from a vendor to a prospective customer asking for more information or clarification concerning the nature of a requested computer system.

Leveled Approach to Documentation An approach to documentation in which a high-level overview is given, followed by a more detailed description, followed by still another more descriptive narrative, until the most detailed level of documentation is reached. With complex systems each level is generally subdivided to simplify the more detailed descriptions.

Live Data A term for information or data that is actually taken from your business. For example, payroll data from your personnel department.

Loosely Coupled See *Coupling*.

Low-Level Language Machine-level and assembly-level languages that are closer to the language that the computer can understand. See *High-Level Language*.

Low Resolution A terminal device (CRT or printer) that cannot print as many dots in a character's dot matrix as a graphics or high-resolution dot matrix device. See *Dot Matrix Printer*.

LPM An abbreviation for lines per minute. LPM is a measurement of the speed in which a printer can operate. For example, 100 LPM is considered slow for a line printer.

Machine Code The computer-readable instructions that are the result of the computer's "reading" (compiling) a computer program. See *Machine-Oriented Computer Language, High-Level Language, Low-Level Language*.

Machine-Oriented Computer Language A low-level computer language, that is, a computer language that is closer to the language of the computer than to the language of people. See *Low-Level Language* and *High-Level Language*.

Magnetic Tape Peripheral-storage device utilizing magnetic tape as the medium. This is usually found on small-business computers only as a way of backing up large hard-disk storage devices. See *Hard Disk* and *Peripheral*.

Management Information Data belonging to the whole spectrum of information used by businesspeople in the performance of the business-management function. Examples would include financial ratios, sales figures, personnel utilization, and equipment downtime.

Master Files The data that is maintained on a computer system to provide a point of posting. For instance, the customer file is the master file for a sales system.

Maxi Computer The large, more expensive computers generally costing $150,000 or more.

Meg A term for megabytes, or one million bytes of information capacity. See *Byte*.

Memory Dump The procedure that allows a programmer to see portions of a program or data that are internal to the computer. Memory dumps are used by programmers to resolve programming errors.

Menu Driven An application or series of programs that presents the user with function choices from which the user is able to "choose from the menu" which function is to be executed next.

Mini Computer A medium-sized computer that is larger than the personal and small-business microcomputers and smaller than the very large business computers. Generally accepted as having a multiuser capacity and costing between $25,000 and $125,000.

Multiple-Application Decision A step-by-step approach or methodology for determining the best proposed software packages for a multiple-application decision. For example, how to determine the best proposal for a combination payroll, accounts receivable, and general ledger system. See *Single-Application Decision*.

Multi-Terminal The ability to have more than one terminal operating on one computer at the same time. Multi-terminal capabilities require both special hardware characteristics and software flexibility.

Needs Analysis Document prepared as an initial step in the process of procuring a small-business computer system. The purpose of this document is to identify those business information requirements that may justify automation.

OEM Abbreviation for Original Equipment Manufacturer. OEMs are companies that buy and manufacture computer components and combine them into a marketable computer product.

On-Request Reports Reports from a computer system that can be printed on the user's request. Often these reports are not printed unless the user requests them.

Operating Constraints Those characteristics of a computer's hardware that place requirements on its environment. Examples include operating temperature and humidity.

Operating Lease A lease agreement in which the lessor is in effect renting the equipment to the lessee for the term of the lease. Ownership of the equipment does not pass to the lessee at the end of the lease term.

Operating System The special set of programs and utilities that control the various parts of the hardware and make it operate as a unit. The user's application programs execute under the control of the operating system. For example when a program prints a line, the function is performed by the operating system, which executes the actual printing at the request of the application program.

Operator's Manual Operations documentation that tells the computer operator how to operate the system and describes the system functions performed.

Output Collectively refers to the reports and screens that are available to the user of a computer system and which allow the user to see the results of calculations and the status of management information.

Pascal A popular computer language that operates effectively and efficiently on microcomputers.

Past-Due Customer List Report showing customers who are past due in paying off an account receivable. The report shows the amount categorized by how late the payment is and any partial payments received.

Percentage of Purchase Price When used in reference to maintenance contracts, this term refers to a monthly maintenance amount that is calculated as a percentage of the total purchase price of the equipment covered by the maintenance contract.

Perforated Paper Special printer paper that is perforated so that it can enter the computer as a continuous paper and can be bursted (separated) into single sheets after printing. Perforations along the outside edges are often used to allow special pin-feed holes in the paper that the printer uses to feed the paper into the printer. With the perforations the pin-feed holes can be torn off.

Peripheral A device that is external to the main frame of the computer. Generally peripherals are used as input or output devices, such as printers, CRTs, and disk drives.

Peripheral Interface See *Controller*.

Point-of-Sale Equipment Equipment used to receive sales information at the time it occurs (for example, at the cash register). This is in contrast to waiting until the end of the day to enter sales information using accumulated sales slips or other documents.

Port An electrical outlet that the computer uses to pass information from the mainframe to the peripheral devices.

Printer A peripheral device that is used to make printed copies of information in the computer.

Program Design and Coding The process of designing, specifying, and writing the logic used by a computer when it performs a programmed task.

Program Documentation The set of documentation that describes the interworkings of all the programs in a software package.

Programming Aids Utilities and tools that a programmer can use to help improve his efficiency. These aids may be physical tools, such as flowchart templates, or automated tools such as high-level language or a prewritten sort program.

Proposal The document prepared by a hardware or software vendor outlining how the vendor's computer system will satisfy the potential buyer's needs. A proposal is generally offered in response to the buyer's request and addresses the needs outlined in the buyer's requirements document. See *Request for Proposal and Requirements Document*.

Punch Card Small heavy paper cards that load information into a computer via punched-hole patterns. Used more frequently in the 1950s and 1960s on large computers.

Purchase/Cash Disbursements Cycle The business cycle in which a purchase is made, a bill is received, an account payable is recorded, and finally the payable is reduced or eliminated when the payment is remitted to the seller.

RAM An abbreviation for *Random Access Memory*.

Random Access Memory Computer memory that can be accessed randomly or directly without accessing every memory location before it. RAM can be altered by a program and is lost when the computer is turned off.

Read Only Memory Computer memory that can be accessed randomly or directly without accessing every memory location before it. Read only memory is permanent memory that contains the basic repetitive operational instructions that the computer needs. The instructions are "burned" into the memory by the manufacturer and cannot be lost, even when the computer is turned off; neither can they be altered by programs.

Request for Proposal A document, generally consisting of a vendor letter and requirements documents, which is sent to vendors to request that they prepare a proposal to meet the customer's needs. See *Vendor Letter* and *Requirements Document*.

Requirements Definition Statement of the requirements a business has for the performance of a computer system. See *Requirements Document*.

Requirements Document A written document that contains the requirements definition. See *Requirements Definition*.

Retail Inventory Method An accounting process for inventory valuation and sales-cost calculation that works on an average-cost basis. This method starts with a base ratio of sales price to cost and uses that to estimate cost of goods sold given total sales at retail.

ROM An abbreviation for *Read Only Memory*.

Sales/Cash Receipts Cycle The business cycle in which a sale is made, an account receivable is recorded, and cash is received to eliminate the receivable.

Sales Deposit Voucher The document that accompanies a deposit of cash receipts and is the source of posting to the accounts receivable ledger.

Shared Processing Sharing the resources of a computer among two or more businesses, departments, or functions.

Single-Application Decision A step-by-step approach or methodology for determining the best proposed software package for a single application such as payroll. See *Multiple-Application Decision*.

Single-Sheet Feed A printer that can print on standard paper, which is not perforated and is not continuous. See *Perforated Paper*.

Small-Business Software Computer programs designed to meet the bookkeeping and management information needs of a small- to medium-sized business.

Software The instructions that tell a computer what to do and how to do it.

Software House A computer company that specializes in developing computer software packages; a programming company that develops application software.

Software Package Set of programs that interact to perform a predefined function. See *Software*.

Source Code The English-like computer instructions that make up a noncompiled computer program. See *High-Level Language* and *Low-Level Language*. See *Compile*.

Special Characteristics When used in reference to a requirements document, this term defines operating characteristics of the desired system. An example would be the need for a printer that can print on standard letter-size paper.

Special Requirements When used in reference to a requirements document, this term designates certain unique characteristics which are desired. An example would be a special report that is needed.

Stop-Credit Report A listing of customers who have met some predetermined criteria for having their credit cut off.

Summary-Level Transactions Transactions that carry summary data found in more detailed transactions. For example, a summary-level payroll transaction may carry the total withholding taxes and total gross pay for all employees in a certain department. See *Detailed Transactions*.

Systems Documentation The set of documentation that gives a complete overview of the software system. The systems documentation generally includes flowcharts showing how data flows from program to program and how the various subfunctions are related.

System Requirements Those characteristics of a system that are necessary for its performance in a particular business environment. See *Requirements Definition* and *Requirements Document*.

Systems Development Methodology An approach or methodology for developing computer systems in a standardized, uniform manner. The methodology outlines each step, such as analyzing the needs, designing the system, performing the programming, testing, converting functions, and training the personnel who must operate the system.

Terminal A peripheral device that can serve as an input device (card reader) or an output device (printer) or both (CRT).

Thermal Printer A printing device that uses a special heat-sensitive paper. Thermal printers are generally cheaper but the thermal paper required is more expensive than standard computer paper.

Tightly Coupled See *Coupling*.

Transaction Driven A term for computer software that is designed to create transactions that are later grouped or batched together to be processed by the next program.

Transactions Records containing new information about the master-file data and which are used to update the master-file data. For instance, sales transactions are posted to customer master files on a computerized sales system. See *Master Files*.

User's Documentation The documentation that explains to the end user what the system can do for each user and how to prepare input and instructions so the system will perform the proper functions. See *End User*.

Vendor Evaluation Sheet A document prepared to allow comparison of the characteristics of various vendor proposals.

Vendor Letter The letter a prospective buyer sends to a computer-system sales organization. The letter contains the specifics of the desired software and hardware along with guidelines for responding.

INDEX

A

Accounting cycles:
  general ledger, 27, 28
  inventory, 27
  payroll, 27, 28
  purchases/cash disbursements, 27, 34
  sales/cash receipts, 27, 34
Accounts receivable, 27
Accounts payable, 27

B

Building costs, 135

C

Candidate for automation, 31
Canned programs (see Packaged programs)
Capital leasing, 142
Characters per second, 49, 53
Comment statements, 82
Controller, 50, 51
Conversion, 137

Costs:
  building, 135
  hardware, 141–143
  maintenance, 135–137, 143
  obsolescence, 135–136
  personnel, 134
  software, 141–143
  training, 134
Coupling, 127, 128, 130
CP/M, 42
CPS (see Characters per second)
CPU, 48, 49, 53
CRT, 47, 53
Cycles, accounting (see Accounting cycles)

D

Daisy wheel printer, 50, 53
Data processing trends:
  1950's era, 4–6
  1960's era, 6, 7
  1970's era, 7, 8
  1980's era, 8, 9
Decision matrix, 124–126, 128–130
Demonstration, 21, 113–115

159

Index

Depreciation, 141
Disk drive:
   controller, 51, 52
   floppy disk, 3, 9, 51
   hard disk, 4, 9, 52
   peripheral interface, 51, 52
Documentation:
   operations, 85, 86
   program, 82–85, 90
   systems, 78, 90
   user, 77, 90
   walkthrough, 86, 88
   what to look for, 87, 88
Dot matrix printer, 3, 9, 49, 50

E

Eight-step purchase process, 13–16
End users, 89
Enhanced graphics, 51
Error code table, 88, 89
Evaluation of vendors (see Vendor evaluation)

F

File layouts, 85
Floppy disk, 3, 9, 51

G

General ledger cycle, 27, 28
Generic packages, 28, 33
Graphics, 51

H

Hands on experience, 86, 89
Hard disk, 4, 9, 52
Hardware:
   components (figure), 46
   costs of, 141–143
   CPU, 48, 49, 53
   CRT, 47, 53
   disk drive, 51, 52
   independence of, 42
   keyboard, 47, 48
   printer, 49–51
   vendors, 71, 73
Hidden costs, 131–138
High resolution monitor, 47, 53

I

Interfacing, 22, 63, 72
Investment tax credit, 141
Inventory cycle, 27

K

K (see Kilobyte)
Keyboard, 47, 48
Kilobyte, 48

L

Leasing, 142
Letter of inquiry, 101, 109
Letter to the vendor (see Vendor letter)
Lines per minute, 49, 53
Low resolution monitor, 47, 53
LPM (see Lines per minute)

M

Maintenance costs, 135–137, 143
Maintenance agreements, 143–145
Management information, 29, 34
Master file, 21, 22
Meg (see Megabyte)
Megabyte, 51, 54
Memory:
   kilobyte, 48
   random access, 48, 49
   read only, 48, 49
Memory dump, 5, 9
Microcomputers, 123
Minicomputers, 123
Monitor:
   color, 47
   high resolution, 47
   low resolution, 47
Multiple application decision, 127–129, 130
Multiple-terminal, 134

N

Needs analysis, 16, 28–30, 34
Number entry pads, 48

O

Obsolescence costs, 136

OEM (*see* Original equipment manufacturer)
Operating lease, 142
Operating system, 41, 42
Operations documentation, 85, 86
Operator's manual, 77, 85, 89
Original equipment manufacturer, 7, 9

P

Packaged programs, 6, 9, 27, 28, 69, 106, 109
Payables (*see* Accounts payable)
Payroll cycle, 27, 28
Peripheral equipment, 53, 137–138
Peripheral interfaces, 51, 52
Personnel costs, 134
Point-of-sales equipment, 29, 34, 95, 98
Printer:
   characters per second, 49, 53
   daisy wheel, 50, 53
   dot matrix, 3, 9, 49, 50
   enhanced graphics, 51
   graphics, 51
   lines per minute, 49, 53
Program documentation, 82–85, 90
Program specifications, 82
Proposal, 101, 109
Purchase process (*see* Eight-step purchase process)
Purchases/cash disbursements cycle, 27, 34

R

RAM (*see* Random access memory)
Random access memory, 48, 49
Read only memory, 48, 49
Receivables (*see* Accounts receivable)
Record layouts, 85
Reliability, 123
Request for proposal, 19, 93, 98, 104, 109 (*see also* Vendor letter)
Requirements definition, 22, 57, 58, 65

Requirements document, 17, 60–65, 72, 101
Resolution, 51
RFP (*see* Request for proposal)
ROM (*see* Read only memory)

S

Sales/cash receipts cycle, 27, 34
Shared processing, 6, 9
Single application decision, 124–126, 130
Single-sheet page feed, 50
Software:
   demonstration, 21, 113–115
   multiple application decision, 127–130
   packages, 6, 9, 27, 28, 69, 106, 109
   program documentation, 82–85, 90
   program specifications, 82
   purchasing, 141–143
Source code, 77, 78, 90
Systems documentation, 78, 90
Systems requirements, 58

T

Terminal, 47, 54
Training costs, 134
Transaction, 21, 22
Transaction driven, 6, 9

U

User (*see* End user)
User documentation, 77, 90

V

Vendor demonstration, 113–118
Vendor evaluation, 99
Vendor letter, 18–19, 22, 93–98
Vendor list, 18, 72

W

Walk through, 86, 88

NOW . . . Announcing these other fine books from Prentice-Hall—

To order these books, just complete the convenient order form below and mail to **Prentice-Hall, Inc., General Publishing Division, Attn. Addison Tredd, Englewood Cliffs, N.J. 07632**

SO YOU ARE THINKING ABOUT A SMALL BUSINESS COMPUTER

R.G. Canning and N.C. Leeper

Specifically designed for the businessperson with little or no knowledge of computers, this book gives step-by-step guidelines for selecting a small computer system and for using it effectively in daily office routines. Includes definitions of common computer terms and a list of leading computer suppliers.

$18.95 (hardcover) $10.95 (paperback)

HOW TO MICROCOMPUTERIZE YOUR BUSINESS

Jules A. Cohen and the Staff of Orbis

A complete guide to selecting data processing equipment and services, this book shows how to plan a computer system tailored to the needs of any business. Emphasizing the managerial decisions essential to computerization, the authors tell how to decide if a computer fits in with business objectives, and more.

$18.95 (hardcover) $9.95 (paperback)

Title	Author	Price*
_____	_____	_____
_____	_____	_____
_____	_____	_____

Subtotal _____

Sales Tax (where applicable) _____

Postage & Handling (75¢/book) _____

Total $ _____

Please send me the books listed above. Enclosed is my check ☐ Money order ☐ or, charge my VISA ☐ MasterCard ☐ Account # _____

Credit card expiration date _____

Name _____

Address _____

City _____ State _____ Zip _____

Prices subject to change without notice. Please allow 4 weeks for delivery.